MY little BLACK BOOK TO SUCCESS

REACH, TEACH, AND SEND

MY little BLACK BOOK TO SUCCESS

Tom Marquardt
The Profit Repairman®

TATE PUBLISHING & *Enterprises*

My Little Black Book to Success
Copyright © 2008 by Tom Marquardt. All rights reserved.

This title is also available as a Tate Out Loud product. Visit www.tatepublishing.com for more information.

No part of this publication may be reproduced, stored in a retrieval system or transmitted in any way by any means, electronic, mechanical, photocopy, recording or otherwise without the prior permission of the author except as provided by USA copyright law.

This book is designed to provide accurate and authoritative information with regard to the subject matter covered. This information is given with the understanding that neither the author nor Tate Publishing, LLC is engaged in rendering legal or professional advice. Since the details of your situation are fact dependent, you should additionally and independently seek the services of a competent professional. It is written with the understanding that the author is not giving legal, financial, and/or other professional advice, but of personal experience that has helped to change the life of the author. He wishes only to share his information, so that small and mid-sized businesses might prosper.

In this narrative, the masculine gender is used to refer to both men and women with the sole intent of readability. No gender discrimination implications are intended.

The opinions expressed by the author are not necessarily those of Tate Publishing, LLC.

Published by Tate Publishing & Enterprises, LLC
127 E. Trade Center Terrace | Mustang, Oklahoma 73064 USA
1.888.361.9473 | www.tatepublishing.com

Tate Publishing is committed to excellence in the publishing industry. The company reflects the philosophy established by the founders, based on Psalm 68:11,
"The Lord gave the word and great was the company of those who published it."

Book design copyright © 2008 by Tate Publishing, LLC. All rights reserved.
Cover design by Jacob Crissup
Interior design by Kellie Southerland
Edited by Tracy Terrell

Published in the United States of America

ISBN: 978-1-60462-535-6
1. Business & Economics: Business Development: Small Business: Management
2. Business & Economics: Sales: Techniques
08.02.05

IN LOVING MEMORY OF MY BIG BROTHER, SCOTT ALLEN, WHO WATCHED OVER ME WHILE HE WAS HERE ON EARTH, NOW FROM ABOVE. YOU WILL NEVER BE FORGOTTEN.

DEDICATION

This book is dedicated to every person who has made a difference in my life and in my future: my mother, Lynn; my entire family; the team at Platinum; my best friends for life, Matt, Jim, and Scott; Rebecca, Nick, and Kayla; and the Tate family and their wonderful publishing team! It is also dedicated to everyone out there that has a lemonade stand as their side business. I have been able to make so much lemonade out of my life's lemons, that after I get finished with this book, I am opening up a second, much larger lemonade stand to turn a healthy little profit out of that additional lemon juice. *If your stand is open and ready for business, then turn the page, sit back, and enjoy the next few hours. We win as one!*

I would like to thank you for the time and consideration that you will take in reading my book and joining me in my mission of increasing the success rate of small and mid-sized businesses. I welcome you and look forward to hearing any comments and/or thoughts that you may have. If you would like to be included as a testimonial or case study in my upcoming book series in which you have used this book and/or any of my product service lines to create greater success, please contact me so we can discuss the possibilities.

I am personally available for you and/or your organization in the following service capacities:

- Customized corporate and group programs and workshops

- Associate training and teaching on all levels

- Keynote address and specialized speeches

- Motivational speaking on leadership, teamwork, communication, and peak performance

- Sales and operational-driven solutions

- On a complete consulting basis, determined by each client company's wants and needs.

TABLE OF CONTENTS

11	Introduction
13	Part 1: Stop Biting Your Nails and Start Sharpening Your Claws!
17	Section 1: Stop Doing X and Start Doing Y
29	Part 2: Run Your Business Like a Hotel!
31	Chapter 1: "A" Operations
79	Chapter 2: "$\sum$" Sales and Marketing
121	Chapter 3: "∞" Human Resources
133	Chapter 4: "Ω" Accounting
145	Epilogue

INTRODUCTION

Welcome. My book is not very long because I believe that actions mean more than words, and I want you to have more time to start your actions than reading my words.

My goal is to do three things for my mission of increasing small and mid-sized businesses' success rates:

Reach

Teach

Send

I want to *reach* as many small and mid-sized businesses as I can. I want to *teach* every small and mid-sized business owner and associate, rock-solid, time-tested principles for individual and company success. I want to *send* small and mid-sized businesses in motion with concrete, corrective action plans to implement *today*, so that the owners and associates have a tomorrow to look upon.

I want to take a moment and ask that while you are reading my book, you do two things: First, believe in yourself as an element of change within your life's structure. *You can* make that difference. Second, understand that taking yourself too seriously about learning new ideas will not help make the idea of believing in them any stronger.

I must tell you that this book started out as a little diary for myself, while working and consulting for various small and mid-sized businesses, and turned into a book that can offer direction and techniques with proven blueprints for implementation to be successful in your life, as well as your career. The book's call to action to you, the reader is: "Learn from your past, work today, formulate action plans for tomorrow." *Live by it!*

PART 1
STOP BITING YOUR NAILS AND START SHARPENING YOUR CLAWS!

I would like you to take ten minutes, and ten minutes only, and write down the top five items that you worry and/or are fearful about on a continuous basis in the space provided below.

_____
_____
_____
_____
_____

Good. Now that you just remembered what your top five worries and/or fears are, you are now fully ready to transform them into an element of change for your success, even with that "bad feeling" in the pit of your stomach saying, "*Stop!*"

Worries and fears can never go away, and in fact, if someone says that they do not have any worries or fears, then they have nothing to lose, and we all have something to lose, be it monetarily, physically, emotionally, and/or spiritually.

I am not here to tell you how to get rid of your worries and fears. Instead, I want you to learn how to neutralize them and utilize the fourteen points listed on the following pages, so that, on a daily basis, you can channel your extra energy from not worrying to producing results that start your upward mobility into being greater than even you thought that you could or should be. Once you do that, worries and fears will seem to fade away.

Do you remember when you were a teenager? What were your worries and fears then? Are those same fears still present, or have most of them faded away for new ones that adulthood brought on? By neutralizing worries and/or fears with my stop doing

"*X*" and start doing "*Y*" section, you are breaking the chain of being unproductive, so you can stop biting your nails and start sharpening your claws.

SECTION 1: STOP DOING X AND START DOING Y

X 1: Stop focusing on tomorrow.

Y 1: Today is everything. If you focus on *today*, today will be tomorrow and tomorrow will be your *everything*. You are your own change element.

X 2: Stop making the first thought of your day negative.

Y 2: How many times do you set your alarm clock and think, "I do not want to wake up that early," or "How early do I have to get up?" But if this is the last thought in your mind before bedtime, that idea festers and plays over and over in your mind throughout the night. When you wake up, you hit that snooze button and say, "Surely it is not tomorrow already." From now on, you need to set the alarm clock and say to yourself, "I cannot wait for tomorrow to come so that I can make a difference in my life and career." When that alarm clock sounds, jump out of bed and walk around for at least two minutes so you do not get back into bed. This will start off your day charging and thinking in your mind about all of the opportunities you have to make a difference.

X 3: Stop putting your concerns first.

Y 3: We are all connected to one another, and each of us relies on hundreds, if not thousands, of people daily to live the way we do at this very moment. How did you get to work? Did you drive? Think for a moment. How many people did it take to dig up the raw materials necessary to make your car? How many people did it take to assemble your car? How many people did it take to produce the gas/energy supply for your car? And how many people did it take to build the road that you drove on to get to work? The list goes on, but you can see the connection forming. Start to see that "your concerns" should mean "our concerns." From that, when you look at a project or a task to complete, ask yourself instead, "How do we succeed?" first, and then you can start to move your success dial for "you."

X 4: Stop breaking the rules.

Y 4: Start realizing that in this "ever-connected-to-database society" that we live in today, you cannot break the system's rules to succeed in the very beginning.

You must follow the rules until you have complete understanding of who, what, why, and how the rules of the game are played. Then you can start the upward trend to enter a plan of success within life and business. Without knowing the who, what, why, and how about the rules of the "game," you will be identified by the system as a renegade and kicked out before the breakaway opportunity presents itself for full fruition to success.

X 5: Stop pushing yourself.

Y 5: Start utilizing your time more wisely.

We are all spacers of time, to some degree. If we were given one hour to do a specific task or job, probability could tell us that we would do that task or job correctly in just fifty-five minutes, with no reduction in quality. If this five-minute savings is true, imagine if you add up those five minutes that you just saved and multiply it by eight hours in your workday. That equals forty minutes more in a workday to become more productive.

Say you took those forty minutes in a working day and multiplied it by five days in a workweek, which would be two hundred minutes a workweek, or three hours and twenty minutes. If we take those two hundred minutes a workweek and multiply it by fifty workweeks a year, that would equal ten thousand minutes or 166 hours and forty minutes a year of greater productivity by utilizing your time more wisely by not spacing your tasks. If you then took 166 hours and forty minutes and divided it by forty hours in a workweek, you would get 4.17 workweeks, or about one month more of time in a year for more available, more productive time.

All you have to do for this "extra" time is stop spacing your tasks and pushing yourself and instead start utilizing your time more wisely. Worst case scenario, what could you do with two more weeks of work accomplished a year? How much more of a success could you be in your position, both financially and status-wise?

But be careful. Do not try to lower your efficiency ratio too much, or you will burn out and hit a wall of reduced results. Instead, focus on each task until the goal is completed the right way and in a timely manner, without spacing involved. Only then will you find under each task some piece of time that came from having your efficiency higher, not your pushing of those efforts, thus producing your extra "time of success."

X 6: Stop thinking that you are equal to everyone else.

Y 6: Start remembering this one simple fact: We are all equal in this world to everyone else on just one thing, no matter who we are or what we do: *time*.

Each of us has exactly twenty-four hours a day, seven days a week, and fifty-two weeks a year to make a difference. What we do with those precious moments makes the difference between success and non-success of those goals and achievements that we want to obtain. By knowing that you are not equal to others, except in your time constraints, you can focus on doing more with that one equal item to gain success over others.

X 7: Stop looking for the quick fix.

Y 7: Start understanding that most good plans to success are not the winning lottery ticket.

You must always set a goal and continuously measure it with reliable statistics and logical data for comparisons, monitoring its progress, and taking corrective actions to get back on track. Achievement is like building a home; it must be pre-planned, budgeted for, executed with daily hands-on management, have managed solutions (contingency plans), and be ready for situations when other ways to achieve the end result must be applied within a finite time frame.

You must always make sure that your foundation is laid correctly and is "rock-solid" before you move on to the next phase of your "finishing schedule/plan." Always keep a fresh visualization of what the finished product/goal needs to look like and have several benchmark signoffs along the way to make sure that you are on pace. Goal achievement does not happen overnight, and a lot of people, both directly and indirectly, come into your life that factor into your achievement or non-achievement of those goals. Depending on others to follow through or play a part in your goals must be an understanding.

You cannot go from A to Z in your goals, without "C"ing that "U-R" going to meet "X" person along the way, who will contribute to or detract from your achievement. Reaction to that exterior catalyst must be planned for, and you must understand that your goals have to unfold, like this book, one page at a time.

"To the World you might very well be one person, but to one person, you might very well be the World to their goals and achieving them."

X 8: Stop your "nos."

Y 8: Start your "knows"!

If you say no to something, ask yourself, "Why did I just say no to that?" Start with knowing *why* you said no before you actually say no, because once you say no, that no may have far-reaching consequences. When you commit to something by saying no to it, and then end up finding out that you could have done it, an opportunity for that action is lost forever. Make sure that each decision you make has been well thought out.

Life has a rippling effect. When you always say no to someone, soon he will start asking someone else, because he really wants a yes from you. But, if every answer you give is yes and you cannot follow through with that yes commitment, soon your word will not hold any credibility, negatively impacting your life and career.

Remember, committing to something too fast is also never the answer 100% of the time. Knowing why you say yes or no to something is the only way to be successful in following through with your commitments. Do you know why you are reading this book? Because, you said yes *to making a difference in your life, career, and increasing the success rate of small and mid-sized businesses!*

X 9: Stop putting "I" in group.

Y 9: Start understanding that anything to do with a group of people becomes part of the group, and the "I" work must be given to the group completely. Even though your overall efforts may be proportionally unfair if your contribution to the task as a whole was greater than the rest of the group members, the end result is that you either succeed or don't succeed as a group, period!

Although as an individual you want to be successful, you automatically decrease your chance to be successful at the group's goals if you focus only on your individual success. The control of the outcome of the group's goal will no longer be solely in your hands. The team must never have anything but one saying: "We win as one." When one individual on your team does not hold up his weight or proportionate responsibilities, you must increase your efforts to make sure that you neutralize this downward trend so that the group can stay on course for success. You must make sure that the team's level does not step down to match the output of the weakest link, but rather the other way around.

If you focus on the team, the remaining team members will respect you, and by doing this, your leadership will come through and more tasks will be afforded to you, which will contribute to your individual success. By leading by example within the group, the group will succeed and, in the end, you will too. If you want to win, you must put away all of the "I" contributions and have a giving, rather than a receiving, attitude. Once that happens, the "I" success will occur.

X 10: Stop talking about action items.

Y 10: Instead, start working all of your action plans to completion before you add more items to your list.

You will only be successful and earn just rewards on the action items that you complete successfully, not on how many you have to do or that you have in a *W.I.P.* (work in progress) file. Obviously, having too few action items is also the wrong answer. Keep a constant gauge on yourself to make sure that task saturation is not creeping up on you. The moment that it is, stop talking about action items and prioritize your outstanding items. Then complete each one of them until you are at a level to devote ample time to any new items.

X 11: Stop thinking that the end result is what matters.

Y 11: Start remembering that every step you take is a step closer to your goal's finish and that the result at the end of your goal's journey is the total effect of all of your little steps before.

These little steps are not the cause of your success, but the reason it occurred. Put more focus on each and every step. When you do this, you can quickly identify if the steps are getting you to your goal or directing you somewhere else, making your end result a failure. Immediate correction can be taken when you focus on each step as you take it. Once you realize that your steps are going in the right direction, you can commit to those steps with confidence and be able to follow through and finish the tasks until you reach the goal. Results will only be seen when all of the steps already taken are tied together as a solid line to form the chain of events needed on each and every goal in order to achieve success.

X 12: Stop the "what ifs."

Y 12: Start taking responsibility for your own actions in all situations, even the ones that you cannot totally control.

If it happened to you, your actions, no matter how small a part that they played in the outcome, are still a part of the outcome; so take that portion of the responsibility without hesitation. There are many factors as to why things happen the way they do. Some of your own actions account for it; some do not. No matter the "what ifs," remember that sitting around and wondering about them will only displace your time and stop you from changing your situation. Stand out of the crowd, accept your situation, and stop questioning, "Why me?" and, "What if?" after you commit to an action of change to resolve the situation. Only then can you execute a plan to change within.

No matter what, you and you alone have the ability to

change your situation. It may not be immediate, but change will happen with an executed plan from a person who has first accepted the reality that it is only his actions that can improve this situation. Taking responsibility for actions in your life is a big step to turn your situation into success.

X 13: Stop wanting things to stay consistent.

Y 13: Start understanding that the only consistent thing in life is change.

If you want something to happen, no matter how little of a movement it is within your life, it will never take shape if you do not first embrace the change element behind it. Change is a great catalyst with a specialty to accelerate events and make all things possible. Once you have that mind-set, you will no longer have the attitude, "*Okay*, what's next to go wrong with this situation?" Instead, you will say, "Great! What's the next opportunity to make, not have, success come to me?"

The flexibility for action that you have when your mind-set is changed to the latter is amazing. When you have the understanding that change is right around the corner, it will give you the edge over the competition, because instead of looking into your life as a constant, stagnant model, you are continuously looking to embrace its metamorphosis into a great opportunity.

By successfully taking the change element and working with it, rather than against it, you will be ahead of the change and its time frame, thus making you more available to capitalize upon it before others, leading to greater success. "Change gives you the ability to rise above and deliver upon command, therefore leading to more positive outcomes." Embrace your change element today for your tomorrow's success!

X 14: Stop reading this book.

Y 14: Start changing your life, both personally and professionally, by taking my written words and product/service lines and turning them in to a lifestyle, not a fad to send you into action.

The difference between success and non-success is in an individual's ability to believe in himself as his own element of change and the daily commitment of that individual with that knowledge of success to execute those changes. Remember, leaders lead and also make mistakes, so the element of change is profitable to a leader and his business. Change and turnover give you the opportunity to evaluate a situation and quickly correct and realign, thus strengthening the whole organization and its future. So, take action today and continue your leadership-driven attitude in your life and career to propel your small and mid-sized businesses' success rate.

PART 2
RUN YOUR BUSINESS LIKE A HOTEL!

Spending most of my life in and out of the hospitality industry (mostly in), I often wondered if the skill set and techniques that I had acquired there could be used in my own personal life and other areas of business to make my mission of increasing the success rate of small and mid-sized businesses a reality. Once I started to implement these principles it was like a secret formula. The formula worked. In fact, it worked very well. This part of the book is for anyone who is a current leader (or who wants to be a leader) in either life or in business. Because small and mid-sized business are the backbone of a country's economy and future growth, we need to start today and turn around their bottom lines, change flat revenue growth, and lower closure and bankruptcy rates so there is a brighter tomorrow for all.

Soon, you will start thinking about your "little boxed world" and how to improve it with the over fifty rock-solid, time-tested principles discussed hereafter as your new "*big box*" to succeed within and outside of your business. If you take just one section out of the following chapters and apply its blueprint to your situation and send it into action, you will produce more positive outcomes.

CHAPTER 1
"A" OPERATIONS

24/7/52

What this phrase means is twenty-four hours a day, seven days a week, and fifty-two weeks a year; this is the operational golden rule to a hotelier. A hotel never closes, which means that it has 525,600 minutes a year to be open and make sure that it operates in the best and most efficient way that it can.

No matter what the posted hours on the doors are for your business, you must be in the mind-set that your business is always "on, open, or alive," 24/7/52. Think of it this way: When your business doors are closed, do potential, current, or future customers (economic decision makers) stop spending their money? Do outside and inside factors affecting your business and your competition stop, or is someone out there creating a better widget than you ending their day when you do? No, he is not!

Obviously, many factors come into play as a big part in determining your operational hours. But when was the last time you truly looked at your business unit's hours with a critical and objective eye and made sure that they were appropriate to make your future goals? Or are those hours just posted for "your convenience?"

If you get into the mind-set that you are always "on, open, or alive," 24/7/52, you will then start to think about how to make the most out of all that "extra" time you have to increase your business' success model. The traditional hours of Monday through Friday, nine to five, are a very antiquated way of thinking. This is a global economy that is always "on, open, or alive," 24/7/52. When you are sleeping, someone from halfway around the world is working.

Your business unit must have a 24/7/52 mentality to be more successful. Only when you embrace this mind-set will new ways "to do more" arise, because you are now always "open" to more success.

YOUR BUSINESS IS MORE PERISHABLE THAN A GLASS OF MILK

For hotel operators, this is a must to understand if they are going to generate the maximum revenue potential on a daily basis. Every night that one single room in a particular hotel goes vacant, that room has lost that night's revenue, forever. It can never regenerate revenue for that given night again, so it becomes non-recoverable potential (left on the table) revenue.

A glass of milk has a longer shelf life than a vacant hotel room. If you do not drink all of the milk that you purchased today, you can at least put that milk back in the refrigerator and have some of it for tomorrow. You can repeat those above steps for at least a couple of weeks, so that you have the opportunity to receive the greatest consumption relationship to the money spent, for the value of that product. Not so for an empty hotel room or for whatever product or industry that you work in. Once that day is gone, you can never sell or use that moment again for revenue generation or operational efficiency gain. With that being said, it means that every business is more perishable than a glass of milk. The business unit that you are involved in must make sure that it has a greater sense of urgency regarding this principle and acknowledge its perishable nature.

Let's say that you have eight hours to make the most money on any given day. After just one hour of that day, you have lost the opportunity of making the maximum revenue generation by 12.5% and counting. Start thinking about how perishable your product really is, even if it has a shelf life of one hundred years. Every day that you do not maximize your revenue potential or gain greater operational efficiency is a day that is lost forever.

Is your business running? *You better go catch it and make the most money with it; it is not a glass of milk!*

INSTALL YIELD MANAGEMENT FOR REVENUE MAXIMIZATION

Hotels talk about their REV.PAR, which stands for revenue per available room, as a driving factor for good room revenue yield management markers. In plain terms, yield management is the study and implementation of techniques to drive and maximize the dollar spent on something in this world into your bottom and top lines.

In theory, there is only a finite dollar amount that is going to be spent on any item or service at any one time. Yield management works to make sure that you get a greater portion of that finite dollar into your business's bank account.

The main points that a hotel focuses on for yield management strategies are simplified below (these are not as detailed as they could be for hotel use), and I will discuss some ways that yield management can make more revenue by applying these core principles to your business unit's settings and implementing your own unique yield management strategies. Once you see how hotels view and implement yield management techniques, you can then modify those broad action items into customized techniques for your own distinct business model, or *call me* and I can help customize them for you.

One way that a hotel makes sure they have good room revenue is through hotel reservations. These reservations can be on a "six p.m. courtesy hold" or on a "guaranteed for late arrival" status. A "guaranteed for late arrival" reservation means that the hotel takes your credit card information and charges that credit card even if you do not show up.

There is a fine line and a continuously changing mixture between having every reservation guaranteed and/or on a six p.m. courtesy hold for a hotel's inventory/room supply on any given night. If a hotel has too many six p.m. courtesy hold reservations, then when 6:05 p.m. comes, and no one shows up for those reservations, that hotel has held rooms out of its general inventory "for sale" for "X" number of days that they could have had those same rooms guaranteed or sold through the group sales department. If the above cancellation of a six p.m. reservation scenario happens at a hotel, then the hotel would have to rely on walk ins/same day reservations and spill over from the competition filling up to cover the void of those remaining unused rooms. A typical hotel usually does very few six p.m. courtesy holds for their total reservation count on any given night, unless they are very slow. On slow days, any reservation is better than no reservation, because the hotel at least has a "soft" commitment from a customer. The probability of customers showing up at the hotel increases if they feel as if they have given a commitment to "do" or "buy."

The theory to apply for your business unit's model when talking about hotel reservations is that you must make sure that your product/service/widget has some sort of accumulating future sales/reservations/pre-sales activity, so you have a greater degree of likelihood that your cash flow will actually come into the business model on any given day. When you have these future sales/reservations/pre-sales, you can then have some sort of future number to place within a forecasting model for tracking cash flows and sales trending. In fact, in hotels the common practice is to have their room reservations overbooking their total inventory by at least 5% over the total available supply for that given day, a week or so forward from the date of the reservation being taken. Hotels even overbook more than 5% for booking dates that are farther out. Hoteliers know that the farther the reservation date is from the time that the customer makes the reservation, the lower the probability that someone will show up, and then hotels can increase their overbooking percentages accordingly.

Hotels can overbook because they have tracked their historical and future reservations, and they know the trends within those requested reservation dates. Probability tells a hotelier that less than 100% of today's reservations will show, unless it is a special event; so why not overbook the hotel to help increase the chance of reaching that 100% occupancy goal? By installing some sort of module for future sales/reservations/pre-sales tracking, your business unit's future cash flows can be trended, thus ensuring a brighter future for your success.

The next yield management techniques are items that you need to know to be successful in rate optimizing and possible discounting decisions. Everyone is familiar with a hotel charging a "room rate" to you when you rent a hotel room, but have you ever heard of your room rate being called a "rack rate"? A "rack rate" is a base rate that is set at an "X" dollar amount by each hotel. This "rack rate" changes for each hotel, but think of the "rack rate" as a starting point of something, so you can measure its progress, both positive and negative, from that "X" point.

Your business unit needs to establish a baseline price point; this "rack rate" should be the optimal price that *you* want to sell your product/service for. Once the "rack rate" is set, thereafter all rates are based off of its mark. In simplistic terms, any room rate above "rack rate" is good, and vise-versa. Hotel example: special events like the Indy 500 in Indianapolis have rates called "Over Rack Rate/Special Event Pricing" during this time period. Due to the special nature/high demand of the dates requested and the limited availability in the area, the hotel room price is very high over the established "rack rate" during that time period. Changes to market conditions may require your "rack rate" to go up or down on an ongoing basis, because it can be a floating price point. But, without setting a "rack rate" for your business model, or the optimal price point that you would like for someone to pay for your product/service, you will never know if someone is paying less or more than what you want to receive for it.

Before you quote your pricing structure for any product/service, first establish your own set of "rack rates." Once you establish a "rack rate," you can then focus on maximizing these rates through rate optimizing. Rate optimizing is used everywhere, such as buying an airline ticket. The end result of rate optimizing in the airline industry is that some people will pay more and some will pay less for the exact same plane ride, to the exact same destination. A lot goes into determining a yield management rate optimizing strategy, but one thing is clear. The goal is, "How do I make the *most* revenue from the finite demand dollars on my finite product/service?" If you are always busy because you have the lowest rates in town for a product/service, is that the best for your business? Would you not rather be 85% busy, but make more revenue than being at 100% capacity? *Yes*!

To make sure that rate optimizing is successful in your business unit's model, you must have three key factors: your baseline "rack rate" established, break-even point on costs, and knowledge that there is a finite supply and market demand for your product/service at any one time. Only by understanding these three key factors can you make a decision to apply discounting techniques or rate optimizing to drive your top-line revenue.

Discounting under your "rack rate" can be a way to drive the total gross sales for your business higher than before, just as long as you remember not to give a discount to everyone on everything. This action of discounting can lower your perceived value to the customer after long periods of time and also consume your finite supply, thus displacing higher-rated business sales.

"Let the customer tell you what you are worth; they will." One person's perceived value of your product/service line(s) is completely different from that of another. Only by asking for the sale and tracking the success rate of getting your "rack rate" will you see pricing trends emerge.

Another way to help your yield management techniques is understanding when, how, and why a consumer buys a product/service within your business unit. Once a traceable pattern of when, how, and why can be uncovered from your customers, sales and marketing campaigns can be developed and implemented to educate these consumers with those product/service demands about you, thus gaining greater market share and raising your revenues.

If you cannot even answer one of the above questions (when, how, and why), then your business model may be going in a direction that could be counterproductive to your success. When is the last time that you put marketing codes on your promotions? How much money did you spend on your last sales and marketing campaign? What was your return on investment on those sales and marketing dollars, and was it a revenue generator or a heavy expense? How much money does it take to acquire a new customer? If you have the knowledge of when, how, and why, then your answers to the above questions would be more concise and clear.

In other words, how can your business prosper if you have no idea where you are today with the questions of when, how, and why your current and/or future customers are buying and/or are not going to buy your product? Understanding the demographics of the people who have a demand for your product and tracking the source (the point when the customer first knows that they want and/or need your product line), along with the denials of those sales is the easiest way to find information on the when, how, and why a consumer buys and the who and where they are coming from to buy it. When you combine the previously mentioned items, an effective yield management strategy for revenue maximization will form and produce lasting results for your business unit.

PENNIES REALLY DO ADD UP

I remember a story told to me as a young boy. It goes like this: In a far off land, many years ago, there was a very poor man that went in front of a king of a very rich land and offered to work for the king for that day for just one penny, and if the king liked his work, the poor man would continue to work for the king every day after that first day for a total of thirty consecutive days.

The only contingency to this payment plan for the king was that for every day that went by that the poor man worked, the king would have to double the poor man's previous days wage from the first day's wage of one cent for thirty consecutive days. After those thirty days, the king would then pay the poor man in full for his thirty days of labor (example, day 1=.01, day 2=.02, day 3=.04, day 4=.08 and so on). Well, the king just knew that he had a sucker in front of him. He thought that he could get the poor man to do a lot of work for him without paying him very much money.

Do you know what happened next? At the end of those thirty days, the poor man made $5,368,709.12 a day and the king owed him $10,737,418.23, due in full at the end of the thirtieth day! The king forgot the exponential factor of the money doubling and never asked about what the poor man was earning daily throughout the month, because to the king, a penny meant very little and could never add up to any *real* amount of money.

The story ends like this: the king was broke, the poor man rich, and the moral of the story is that a penny really does add up. So focus your attention on each penny within your business unit.

If you save just two widgets a day by training the staff not to waste those widgets, and those widgets cost fifteen cents each, you would save $109.50 a year. This would be just the tip of the iceberg for savings within your business. There is a penny to save here and a penny to save there. Just look around, and when you are done, over time, that penny will multiply to thousands of dollars a year that your business unit can bring down to the bottom line, by simply remembering that "A penny really does add up!"

APPEARANCE BECOMES PERCEPTION

It's an old saying that is so true: You never get a second chance to make a good first impression. Why so? Because in today's society, the perceived value of anything is quickly assessed and labeled, even if the truth be told afterward is different. Your business must display a perception and values of: courtesy, respect, responsiveness, understanding, professionalism, and superb service (*CRRUPSS*) to each and every customer up front, or you will never get an opportunity to demonstrate it on a long-term basis to any future clients.

What would be your first impression of the appearance of your operational and sales business units? If it is not good, take action and make it better, and if it is good, make it great. Even if a customer never sees some of the areas within your business units, your associates do, and they will respond with their own perception that your business has courtesy, respect, responsiveness, understanding, professionalism, and superb service to their wants and needs within their workplace. Thus, the associates will start understanding that you are setting the bar higher by having a great appearance. The greater your customer's perception is regarding the appearance of the operations and sales units, the greater the probability that the "first sale" from that customer will take place and continuously grow for you.

CLEANING IS THE CHEAPEST WAY TO MAKE THE "WOW" FACTOR

The most affordable way to "wow" a customer into giving you that selling opportunity is through cleanliness. Cleanliness is a core value that everyone can relate to and associate with. It shows discipline, attention to detail, and follow-through.

If you can demonstrate to a current and/or potential customer that your business unit can excel on the basic level of a core value that cleanliness brings, then the customer will be more willing to include your product into his buying decisions. You can win over a loyal customer by the cleanliness factor, and you don't have to spend a lot of money doing it.

Clean, clean, and clean can mean green, green, and green (money) to your bottom line. Just walk into any business around; let's say that it is a middle-priced establishment for that product that you want. Once you are there for a little while, you receive great service from an associate, and then you walk into their bathroom. The bathroom that they furnish has every necessity needed, but it is dirty, so dirty that it makes you sick to your stomach. What would you think about going back there again? Would you go to another middle-priced establishment for that same product line and keep going back to them if everything was very clean and the service was just as good as the other establishment?

By cleaning your business unit, you are sending a silent, but powerful, message to your current and potential clients about the business unit's core values and the delivery of them. With cleaning costing just a fraction of what it would be to find a new customer, would you not want to have your silent "wow" effect a positive one through cleanliness?

INSTALL S.O.P.S

What is an *S.O.P.*? A standard operating procedure, or an *S.O.P.*, is a blueprint of how to (and much more) on a specific position as a whole and/or a task within that position/item. *S.O.P.*s can be in written, oral, and "shown by example" form, but the most effective version is the written format. Each business unit/person can design his own *S.O.P.*s to fit the desired outcome for each task assigned.

The goal of an *S.O.P.* is to specifically spell out the following (these items below are not always in every *S.O.P.* or in this exact order, depending on what the *S.O.P.* is about, but this will give you a well-rounded understanding of them): when, what, and how to do something, why you are doing this action, how long it takes, what physical actions are required, what the outcome/output will be, and who is responsible.

By having *S.O.P.*s in place, you have a benchmark to gauge an associate and/or a product's statistical performance with. *S.O.P.*s also create the following: training tools to help on-board associates correctly with no "hand me down, bad habit training;" greater consistency in the product, a how to step-by-step manual, so when turnover occurs, you do not have "knowledge drain" on your business unit for that task; unbiased, preset expectation levels on task completion; and a useful baseline value for that task, so you can perform forecasting, efficiency, and budget-modeling projections.

Start looking around your business unit and take action today. If something were to happen to you, who would know what to do and how to do your job the exact and correct way, or even ten individuals' jobs? By installing *S.O.P.*s, this problem is solved. Having *S.O.P.*s is just one more way to protect your business unit's revenue stream. When you install *S.O.P.*s, you can even build greater teamwork. After you install the initial *S.O.P.* on a task, challenge your team members to make those *S.O.P.*s more effective and efficient. You must "build that first mousetrap before you can make it better."

By first building your *S.O.P.*s, you are making that *S.O.P.* available to be enhanced from input by the team. Thus, *S.O.P.*s offer many more benefits to your organization than you can even imagine. In fact, instead of making your business unit micromanaged, *S.O.P.*s create a doorway to a macro environment of teamwork, performance, and revenue-generating attitudes.

An example from the hotel business on a *S.O.P.* is that hotels install *S.O.P.*s for cleaning dirty laundry. The hotel does a *S.O.P.* on how, what, when, and where to do the laundry and how many minutes it should take on an average to fold and clean all of that day's laundry. Cleaning the dirty laundry is *very* critical to a hotel and its success. By installing *S.O.P.*s on the laundry, the hotel can ensure that the laundry's cleanliness and quality is up to expectations, that its labor costs are in line, and they can bring good revenue down to the net operating income.

For your business to be more successful when it installs *S.O.P.*s, prioritize the business from the revenue-generation tasks down to the administrative ones. When you first focus on the task(s) that are directly and proportionately greater than the rest and are affecting your revenue, work backward; then your *S.O.P.s* will have a greater impact on your bottom line in less time. Always think to yourself, "How is my revenue made, and how can I manage it better through *S.O.P.s*?"

INSPECT WHAT YOU EXPECT

We are all humans, not machines, so the one hundredth widget does not look exactly like the first one in most cases. Due to this fact, if we want consistency, standards, compliance, and uniformity, all of which can help breed success for any product, you must inspect the operations and sales aspects of that business.

By doing inspections on the business unit's functions, you can reinforce *S.O.P.s* within the expectations, identify items that do not meet acceptable expectation levels, have an opportunity to realign and correct the unacceptable levels of those identified items, gathering data from which to do analysis for uses of forecasting, efficiency, and budget-modeling projections, and identify your strengths and weaknesses within your business units for management decision and actions.

As your frequency goes up in your inspection cycle, so will your consistency, standards, compliance, and uniformity, but there is a limit of diminishing returns on that cycle of frequency, so try to find the right balance for your business unit when doing inspections.

O.Q.P.L. YOUR PRODUCT

O.Q.P.L. stands for overall quality performance level. Within your business unit, you need to have some sort of established criteria for the quality performance levels of each task that will meet your business unit's output expectations.

By establishing the quality (caliber, class, grade) with the performance (accomplishment, achievement, fulfillment) to the levels (goal, aim, target), your business unit can then determine if those certain tasks are in compliance with your output expectations.

O.Q.P.L. acts as the overseeing agent of that *S.O.P.*, and this action will send a checks and balances approach to the output expectation's success. Once your business unit has *O.Q.P.L.*s in place, the last thing you must determine is what your response will be when the *O.Q.P.L.* determines that those activities are not meeting the output expectations.

DO A YEARLY Q AND A

When was the last time you had a true yearly *Q and A* (quality and assurance) inspection on your business unit's *S.O.P.*s, compliance issues, and rules and regulations? If you did, was it from an independent representative who had a third-party approach to grading and evaluating the outcome? The old saying that you "cannot see the forest for the trees" is exactly what happens to a business unit while they are in the middle of running their "business" and trying to perform self-run/internally generated *Q and A*'s.

When a business unit's operation is live, *S.O.P.*s and protocols sometimes slip through the cracks when accomplishing the end result. When you have somebody from the outside who is neutral to the *Q and A*'s outcome, with familiarity of your industry and specific standards, he can be unbiased and effectively evaluate performance. Thus, by utilizing this outside inspector, your business unit can receive an honest report/scorecard on where it stands today and where the need to improve is for tomorrow's success.

By adding yearly *Q and A*'s as a calendar event, you provide a way to get your business unit driven to a new, higher level, by making the internal factor of wanting to surpass the last *Q and A*'s final "score" as a gauge on how much progress each department has gained, and along the way, protect the business unit's bottom-line profits.

SAFETY AND SECURITY

Several books could be written on these two subjects alone. But instead, I want to stress the importance that these two subjects bring to a successful business unit's survival.

If you do just one thing, please go through and verify adequate safety and security measures within your business unit are in place. Preventative, concurrent, and post-operating safety and security procedures create an area of three-way protection for consumers, associates, and the profit margin. If you have inadequate safety and security procedures, any one of these three areas can be exposed, which will open up a *big can of legal worms*, possibly closing your business unit forever.

Stop reading and go review your safety and security procedures today. This book can wait; it will be here tomorrow, but without having adequate safety and security measures installed, your business may not!

PREVENTATIVE MAINTENANCE

Preventative maintenance, or *p.m.*, as we call it in the hotel industry, is a must to help lower your replacement costs and prevent possible operations and sales breakdowns that can affect your bottom line.

What do I mean by *p.m.*? Well, in the hotel business it means some of the following actions: scheduled coil cleaning of the heating, ventilation, and air conditioning units; bed mattress turning/rotating; cleaning/removing the sediment within the bottom of the hot water tanks; winterizing the exposed piping; caulking tub surrounds; shampooing the carpet, etc. The pattern of *p.m.* is this: tighten the screws, bolts, and belts; oil the lubricated moving parts; clean out areas that accumulate debris; and check on the status of the normal wear and tear of an item, so there is a proactive approach in maintaining its continued life cycle and use. Let's say a hotel never did any *p.m.*s on its air conditioners and a very hot temperature index weekend occurs. The air conditioning units have not had adequate *p.m.* and may only be running at 30% capacity due to dirty filters and the freon not being recharged.

Will the hotel get complaints? Will it have to refund money, lose future business, increase their utility bill, and have bad "word of mouth" created? The answer to everything is *yes*, but preventative maintenance could have helped to avoid and minimize these above situations.

Preventative maintenance is not limited to mechanical items only. Do a *p.m.* on your human resources and the complete business unit as well. When was the last time you went around and made sure that all of the correct Occupational Safety and Health Administration, Department of Labor, and Equal Employment Opportunity Commission posters were in the right place and current? When was the last time that you made sure your locked storage area was secure and functional? The old saying, "An ounce of prevention can give you a lifetime of protection" is correct when it comes to installing *p.m.* in your business unit. By performing *p.m.* within your business unit(s), you are showing a proactive management style that can lead to lower cost structures through your expenses and growth of your top and bottom lines.

TRIAGE MANAGEMENT

The theory of triage management is simple: you can only do so many actions within a certain time frame with the limited resources available. You must prioritize and make hard decisions on where to focus the finite time and resources on, so you maximize the outcome potential.

Use this as an example. If you are a doctor on the front lines of a battlefield, and you have three patients in front of you: patient one, two, and three. Patient one has non-life threatening injuries, but could get infections if not treated. Patient two has modest injuries, but needs to have surgery soon, or he could die. Patient three (a close friend of your family) is very seriously injured and needs extensive and prolonged surgery that would consume most of the medical supplies available, and after all that, his chances of survival are only 10%. What order would you choose to care for your patients, knowing that there is finite time and supplies and that more injured patients are on their way?

If you were to use the theory of triage management, you would choose to care for your patients in this order: patient two, patient one, and then patient three. Why? Because under the above example of triage management, you must try to keep as many patients alive, along with the knowledge of having finite time, supplies, and demand.

Triage management does not say that the items you did not choose to do first were not important, just not as important for the time frame and resources available for the maximum outcome. Remember to focus on the outcome that you need and to move forward after a decision is made, due to the time frames given, and hopefully, if you are wrong, learn from that situation.

Keep asking yourself daily in your business unit, "Is this the most important thing I need to do right now to maximize the outcome of this task's success rate?"

Even though you may not be on a battlefield, your business unit is always under attack from the competition, and you must make decisions daily using triage management theory to prioritize, so your business unit can live and be successful.

"The needs of the many in a business unit outweigh the needs of the few, when you prioritize." Install some form of triage management theory in your everyday decision-making processes to perform as many actions with your finite time frame and resources available.

YOU ARE IN THE SERVICE INDUSTRY

It does not matter what your product line is, service is the key difference to your success. Service builds a value-added benefit that can increase your client's retention rate and generate a higher asking price for your product line. From the very first sale to the one hundredth repeat sale from a satisfied, retained customer, it is the level and consistency of the service that you provide that allows your revenue streams to grow.

Even if you are working for a company and never see a single customer, are you not offering service within your task list to your own workplace, co-workers, and employer? By making each associate very aware that they have a higher purpose than just doing their task list (but instead delivering the best possible service within their task list), you create a sense of urgency in which every action that they do affects a customer. After you get into this mind-set, you can start under-promising and over-delivering on that service that you give, for every aspect within those assigned tasks.

When you lead by example and put this thought into your routine, there is a synergy that is produced; you realize that the value of the whole organization is dependent upon the service that you produce with everything you do and say. *"Visualize great service—delivery first, all things possible thereafter."*

MULTI-TASKING

This phrase is used a lot, but do you really apply it to your business unit? To a hotel operator, he must always multi-task to be successful. Every phone call that rings could be a reservation, daily bank deposits need to be reconciled with last night's audit, room inspections and subsequent disciplinary action if the room cleaning scores are not passing, extra laundry needs folded because someone called in, and so on. On any given day, a hotelier must be in sales, accounting, human resources, and always has operations to deal with. Do you?

Maybe or maybe not, but no matter, you should take a good look at your business unit and identify what, if any, multi-tasking could be done. That way, each task is completed and can also complement the overall achievement of the other tasks by adding value, while creating more efficiency within the whole process.

By having multi-tasking techniques installed, you are bringing synergy to your business unit's workplace and getting away from one-track work habits. Multi-tasking can foster associate growth and development into greater outcome potentials.

As you are reading this book, are you not reading,

using your sight and brain, and breathing? These distinct tasks all work together to accomplish the continuing action of reading this book. They all complement each other but by no means interfere with the overall success of each stand-alone task. *What tasks can you combine today to be more successful in your business unit for greater efficiency?*

W.I.T.F.M.

What does *W.I.T.F.M.* stand for? This acronym means "What's in this for me?" and you must ask yourself this question before directing your business unit in any certain direction. Why would you ask *W.I.T.F.M.?* Because that is what your associates will be thinking when you implement any revised initiatives.

We are human, so for us to do any action, there must be a want or need involved. No matter how unselfish an action is, we want to make sure that the, "What's in this for me?" will be there to satisfy our wants and needs. If an associate cannot find any *W.I.T.F.M.*, motivation to drive successful completion of that task/action will go down. To have more success in new initiatives, have your *W.I.T.F.M.* answer included in the report when you introduce any new plans. *W.I.T.F.M.* is the justification that goes back to the old business saying, "If the deal is good for you and me, then it is a good deal."

By showing the *W.I.T.F.M.* to the associates up front, they will see more of a win/win situation developed in the beginning, because the outcome and rewards for success rests with all, not just a few. Once your associates see that they are performing these plans for an outcome that can satisfy some part of their wants and needs, motivation to achieve those new plans/initiatives will be greater.

WALK-AROUND, HANDS-ON MANAGEMENT WITH LEADING BY EXAMPLE

Walk-around, hands-on management with leading by example is a powerful management tool. Remember, actions mean more than words and those actions speak louder than those words could ever sound. To lead associates to a business unit's success path, you must first be given the permission of those associates to be their leader. To gain this acceptance and trust, there is no quicker, solid platform than by walking around, being in the associates' "lion's den," seeing what challenges they face, and "rolling up your sleeves" to help them through those challenges. Leading an associate through a situation, with the correct *S.O.P.* for that action, reinforces that you "practice what you preach," and you would not ask them to do an action that you would not be willing to do yourself. You have a built-in, universal language to speak and demonstrate your expectation levels for those tasks, when you lead by example.

Once you can demonstrate to your associates that you do walk around to see what is really happening and can do, not say, actions by being hands-on, leadership platforms for directing associates can be built and allowed to grow, because your associates are permitting themselves to be led and directed by you.

Go be a leader with walk-around, hands-on management. Forget sending a memo to the associates on how to do it; show them yourself!

OWNERSHIP ZONES

Divide your business unit into sectors and assign each team member a portion as his own to care for and improve. By creating these zones, you bring a sense of ownership and accountability to each part of that business unit through extensions of these practices, which will also radiate into all areas of the associates' workplace.

It is shown and time tested that when people have some sort of ownership, even in theory, they are more dedicated to care for that item than if there was no connectional ownership afforded to them at all. When you assign ownership zones, you are giving the associates the ability to make a difference directly and consequently, building pride in that ownership for the good of the entire business unit.

As an example, in the limited service hotel business sector, the front desk clerks make sure that there is organization and cleanliness within the area of the greater front desk space, not housekeeping. Breakfast attendants have the breakfast bar area and so on. It is their "own space" to care for.

By assigning even a small portion of each business unit to the associates through ownership zones, you give them the opportunity to rise above and have more control over the outcome of their assignment. Ownership zones can even create a sense of friendly competition among the other team members and their zones and brings the awareness and expectation levels for caring of one's own zone to a higher level, which benefits everyone.

RELATIONSHIP MANAGEMENT FUNCTIONS

Customer relationship management (*C.R.M.*) tools are everywhere in today's world, but behind that software's programming package in computers and those hard files is something more important to understand about *C.R.M.: "Know thy customer."*

This function of "know thy customer" is all that the *C.R.M.* software does at its core. It allows your business unit to better understand, track, and predict what your current and potential customers' wants and needs are. You may ask yourself, "Do I need to know what my customers want and need?" The answer is *yes*! But do you need software/technology to accomplish this? No and yes, depending on your business.

If your business model is small enough, manually doing *C.R.M.* can get you by. No matter what *C.R.M.*

system you install, make sure that your system's framework includes the following:

- Complete statistical tracking, both historically and with concurrent present day data updating functionality

- Profile information, correspondence storage/usage, and precursors to wants and needs

- Task assignment actions for follow up and flagging directions for future time frames

- Multiple viewing and output options within the database querying

- Easy accessibility, implementation, training, and operating

- Potential forecast modeling on all statistical information regarding the wants and needs

- Flexibility, so customizing the *C.R.M.* application to each unique business unit can be accomplished through the highest efficiency, quickest effective impact, and lowest cost structure

DATABASE MINING

"Junk in is junk out" is so true when it comes to your business unit's database(s). If your information is relevant, accurate, and up-to-date, then mining your database(s) can reap both operational and sales rewards. Once you are sure that relevant, accurate, and up-to-date database files are in your system, you should mine that database on a continuous basis. Make sure that when you have database queries from mining that the following occurs: true comparisons of data, tracking and re-tracking of the trending patterns with those pulled query outputs, action/follow-up action from data pulled, and tracking of the queries to determine the success rate of your decisions that were made based on that mined data. Once you can establish those prerequisites of successful database mining, then database mining is not only profitable, but also necessary to drive future management decisions for operational and sales initiatives.

Mining can be profitable for both in-house and third-party use as a revenue generator. Just make sure that you are totally within legal parameters in doing so. Pay attention to one of the golden rules for databases: "Your client's information is like gold, so rule it wisely." What are you waiting for? *"Go grab those picks and start mining all of that gold in those database fields, you forty-niner!"*

TECHNOLOGY UTILIZATION

Today's software and computers are amazing tools for your business unit to drive profit margins with, but if they are not used to their full capacity, just like one of your team members, that business unit is leaving money on the table. Using technology to drive profits is what smart business units do on a continuous basis. Have you recently done a true inventory of what your business unit's full capacity is on its current technology? If not, I would suggest you do not know how to get to "there" from "here," if you do not know where "here" is first. When you are finished seeing what technology inventory is within your current business unit, envision what you would like for it to do and find out how to get from that current point to that "X" point in the quickest and most affordable way.

Ask the entire team, the marketplace, your customers, and even look at what your competition is doing with their technology. By doing this, you will achieve a reference point of what your wants and needs will be from your business unit's technology. Never stop asking yourself, "Can this technology do this or that, and why so?" Since depreciation on technology is worse than a new car, embrace utilization of your current technology's inventory to its full capacity first, before purchasing new.

Look all around your business unit. Once you can achieve greater utilization from your current or future technology, the greater your business unit will operate and minimize its costs along the way.

IDENTIFY EXPRESS SERVICE POTENTIALS

We live in a world driven by express services, a quick this or a quick that, and we need it "this very moment" kind of mentality. In the hotel business, it was identified that two of the largest opportunities for express services were the checking in and out processes of a customer's hotel stay.

Currently, that express service is done at most hotels in one form or another, but what if you were the first hotel to do it, thirty or so years ago? Would you not have had the competitive advantage to grow your repeat and future guests with by offering this untapped, demanded express service? Would that express service not have set you apart from the rest of the hotels and made a marketing niche available for promoting the difference in your whole product line to that of your competitors without changing the core product line?

Take a look around your business unit, listen to your associates and customers, keep abreast of market trends and your competition, and never stop asking yourself, "Is there an opportunity to convert and deliver this or any process in the operations and sales functions to an express service module?"

Express services can also be in the form of amenities, which we will discuss later in this book. Demand for express services will only increase with this "time crunch" world we live in. By conducting beta testing on potential express services, examining the results, and finalizing the outcome, your business unit can develop an express service to get ahead of the demand curve within your own industry and gain market share doing it.

Once your business unit can identify and implement express service potentials, you will reap the benefits through operations, sales, and eventually monetarily. "Express"ing how your business unit is different today, than that of your competitors, will only add to your core product line and profits for years to come.

DAILY HUDDLE

A daily huddle consists of getting the business unit's team members together at the start of a shift for ten to fifteen minutes and conducting an open discussion with associates on yesterday's historical performance metrics that were achieved, today's operations and sales projections, an educational point, and any situations that you and/or the team believes would be an obstacle to meeting today's top and bottom-line projections.

The time during the daily huddle is a great team-building exercise and a way for different departments to interact and share their own knowledge of the business unit experience/insight. Keep your daily huddle simple, short, to the point, and above all, upbeat and positive. Once the team gets into the habit of a daily huddle as a business unit culture, start delegating the discussions to other team members. This way, the ownership is shared by all, and a variety of presentation styles for the daily huddling will be presented. By having ownership shared, different associates will add diversity so the daily huddles will not develop an environment of stagnant actions and repetitiveness or another "daily task/hoop-jumping requirement."

TALK IN SMILE LANGUAGE AND THE FIVE FOOT (5') RULE

Smile Language is not a science, but it really works. Talk to someone on the phone with a frown on your face and then say the exact same words to them with a smile. When you are done, ask that person on the other end of the phone if they were able to tell the difference in your voice. Having a smile on your face transforms your voice to project upbeat and positive tones and that is how a great first impression is made.

In the hotel industry, every associate is trained that when a guest is within five feet of him, he stops what he is doing, if working (but not with a guest already) or talking with another associate, looks that guest in the eyes, and acknowledges their presence, both verbally and nonverbally.

This action creates two benefits. First, it drives the service element and its perception within the business unit to the consumer; and second, it creates a positive byproduct as a visual deterrent to criminal behavior. For example, if you were staying at a hotel and every time you walked by a hotel associate, he looked you in the eyes and wished you a good day, how would you feel about the service? What if you entered a hotel with premeditated thoughts of committing a crime and three different associates throughout the hotel made eye contact with you and acknowledged your presence? Would you be less likely to commit that crime?

Courtesy is lacking in today's world, and by having your associates talk in smile language and provide service delivery in the form of the five foot rule, your business unit's consumers will notice and recognize that you and your team's focus is on the little things, which in turn will make your service element's perception rise above that of your competitors.

LOCATION, LOCATION, AND LOCATION

This applies to everything regarding your business unit, not just the physical location of your operations. What if your Web site was incorrectly key-word phrased, and then no one could find a link to it with the most obvious words? What if your salespeople were making sales calls in a non-feeder city for new revenue generation? What if your copy machine was located farthest from the person who makes 80% of the copies? What if your help wanted ad for janitorial work went into the executive/management section? In the hotel business, if we placed a tropical ocean resort hotel in the middle of a farm pasture in the Midwest, would it be successful as an ocean resort hotel?

All of these above examples show that with improper location, your probability for a successful outcome decreases. Look around your business unit and ask yourself, "Does this or that belong here or there?" "The mountain must always come to the customer, not vice versa." If you do not position your product line in a convenient location for the consumers and their dollars to spend on your business unit, your competitors will.

NINETY-DAY FORECASTING MODEL

Do you have a forecasting model in place for your business unit's revenue and expenses? There are several forecast models out there for everything "under the revenue and expense sun" that you can think of, but if you have no revenues, you surely do not need to worry about how much profits are going to be made after expenses. So, first install a forecasting model on revenue and all else will flow from that.

Some hotels use what is called a ninety-day forecasting model for their room revenue. This ninety-day forecasting model has a tri-fold benefit. First, it projects what the revenue will be like for ninety days out, as of today's date moving forward. Second, it displays future days' pick up in room demand, thus showing trending and pinpointing yield managing opportunities for revenue growth. Third, the model builds behind itself historical numbers for next year's budgeting and comparison tracking purposes.

As a hotel's ninety-day forecast model moves, it is updated weekly, sometimes daily, in very volatile occupancy-driven hotels. Whatever the time frame that a forecast model updates, each time the forecast model moves forward, it builds historical numbers behind it and blends those historical and forecasted numbers together, so that the accuracy of the forecast model for that forward looking time frame grows sharper and more accurate. Due to this fact, the monthly ninety-day forecast model for "X" month will be much more accurate on the eighteenth day of that month than it was on the third. If you were talking a quarter to date forecast, the third month of that quarter would be more accurate than the first.

No matter what your business unit decides, by installing forecasting models in your business unit, you will bring opportunities for revenue growth, expense reduction, trending, demand pick-ups, and assist management decision-making situations.

TWELVE-MONTH PACING MODEL

Picture a pacing model like the following analogy. Pretend that you want to run one mile on a standard quarter-mile track. If you want to run a five minute mile at the start of your run and after two laps (half a mile) your time is three minutes, then you are pacing to finish behind your goal of five minutes because you are half a minute over for that one half of a mile run. A pacing model's format does not take into account that you could quicken your running pace to make up that time of half a minute over, to finish the mile within those five minutes.

Instead, a revenue pacing model can help your business unit gauge if it is on pace to meet the goals set forth and gives a quick yes or no to the revenue pacing question throughout your goals' time frame. A pacing model is different than a forecasting model, since a pacing model takes your historical numbers to date plus what is pre-sold/reserved and compares that number to where you want to be at the end of your goal, which in turn can inform you if you are on pace to meet those goals in the allocated amount of time, with no variables included in its calculation. Think of a pacing model as a macro model that tells you yes or no to the success of finishing your goal in the time allocated. Thus, on the other side of the spectrum, a forecast model is a micro model that includes details and variables as a predictor of the goal's outcome.

In the hotel industry, some hotels use what is called a twelve-month pacing report on rooms sold to determine if they are going to make their yearly rooms-sold budget. A pacing model gives the hotel an ability to make sure that its rooms that have already sold and its pre-sold rooms will be enough to make the budget at the end of that period. Here is an example. Let's say a hotel's goal is to sell 10,000 room nights from January 1 through December 31 to make its yearly rooms-sold goal. On February 13, the hotel has sold *YTD* 1,000 room nights and has pre-sold/reserved 400 more rooms throughout the remaining year until that December 31 date. Is this hotel on pace to make their budgeted rooms-sold goals by December 31? *Yes*, it is ahead of pace by 222 rooms.

Do you know how that number came into existence? If you take those thirty-one days that have already transpired in January, plus the twelve days in February, it equals forty-three days that have passed for that hotel to sell rooms. Then, divide those forty-three days by 365 days in a year, which equals 11.78% of the year that has transpired. You then multiply 11.78 % times the

10,000 rooms nights that are needed to be sold to make budget for the year, and you get 1,178 rooms that need to be sold/reserved before December 31 to be on pace to make budget as of February 13 (you still have the night of the thirteenth to sell rooms, which is why you use the number twelve).

Next, take your 1,000 rooms sold *YTD*, plus the 400 pre-sold from February 13 through December 31 and subtract it by 1,178. You now get a number that tells you if you are over or under pace by "X" number. In this case, you are over your rooms sold in the pacing model by 222 rooms sold or 18.84% ahead of your pacing model to finish the year at your goal of 10,000 rooms sold. Now replace rooms sold with widgets and apply this twelve-month pacing model to your business unit's settings. The benefits of a macro modeling system gives you a simple yes or no answer to your question, "Is my business unit successfully pacing to make its goals?"

When you can combine a micro and macro system of modeling within your business unit, your future will be more accurate on obtaining goals and achievements. By looking at your business from two different model angles, the critical path to success can be shown more clearly for the business unit.

If you have never been somewhere before, a guide can help get you there easier. That is what forecasting and pacing is all about, getting your business unit moving forward with information that helps map and guide your progress for future destinations/goals.

CHAPTER 2
"Σ" SALES AND MARKETING

REMEMBER THE HOOK

Have you ever been fishing or seen how fishing is done? Without some sort of "hooking" device, very little fish would be caught (most do not just jump into the boat willingly). The same is true in selling your product line. Even when you have the most wanted product around, if you do not inform customers where to buy it (the hook in this example), you will see very little quantity sold. When you think of a hook, remember, it is to grab the client's attention long enough for the sales process to begin between the buyer and seller. The hook is not meant to make anyone buy on the spot (but it could), rather the hook's goal is to have the clients open up their minds and communicate (verbally and/or non-verbally) to you, "I am interested in potentially buying your product. Can you please inform me about it?" This allows you, the salesperson, the opportunity to move the client into a sales opportunity for a purchase.

A hook must be deliberately directed to target the clients that you would like to sell your product line to; there is no "one-size-fits-all" hook, so you want to have multiple hooks designed for your different clients and demographics. Let's take an example of one hotel going after three different clients: corporate, leisure, and tour group. Here are some of the hooks for each:

> *Corporate:*
> *Wi-Fi*
> business center
> double miles/points for staying
> express services
>
> *Leisure:*
> location
> indoor pool
> free breakfast
> children under eighteen stay free in the same room

Tour Group:

> negotiated rate
>
> baggage service
>
> group billing capabilities
>
> welcome reception

All the hooks listed above are different, however, they are coming from the same product line and will target very different demographics. By having different hooks in the marketplace, your business unit increases the opportunity to produce sales across a vast number of potential client demographics. Hooks are not only for your new customers; make sure that your product is using hooks for repeat customers as well. With so many products, promotions, and messages out there for a customer to listen to, make sure that you "reel" them in before someone else does.

Happy fishing!

SCRIPT YOUR DIALOGUE

Why do hotels use scripted dialogues in their sales and operations, and why should you start using them? Scripted dialogues can benefit your business unit in the following ways: consistency; professionalism; assurance that the operational and sales talking points are covered; on-boarding, cross-training associates are effectively accomplished; and objective, clear, and non-derogatory answers that can be discussed to a broad-base spectrum that can be documented and used for legality protection.

Ever make a reservation at a hotel? The reservation screen is actually a fill-in-the-blank script that the hotel uses to capture its requested reservation information. In fact, there are parts within that reservation screen that will not let the reservation agent produce a confirmation number until the required information is completely filled in and correct. Ever call an 800 number for guest relations? Ever get a wake-up call from a hotel? These are all examples of scripting within the hotel business.

Now, focus on your business unit and ask yourself, "What tasks can be scripted to help send my business unit into a proactive approach to talking with the customers and converting that captured time with them into a more qualified database for mining, better close ratios, lower miscommunication experiences, and higher profits?"

Once you identify those scripting opportunities, make sure that there is some sort of ongoing quality assurance program installed and corrective action responses in place to maintain all of the benefits that a "scripted company" can yield for itself.

SALES STAGES AND SOURCE OF BUSINESS REPORTS

A way to gauge if your future sales are moving through a sales pipeline successfully (the movement from initial client or prospect contact with your business line to the final sale) is if you convert each of the different events of that sale leading up to the customer giving you his final commitment into sale stages, so you can gauge the progression from the initial sales stage (contact) to the final one (purchase).

Just like any business system, if you break up the chain of events that lead to the end result, the study of each link in the chain can yield more data than just what the starting and ending results show. Each link can show progress throughout, thus leading to opportunities for solution-added methods, plus analytical, statistical, and historical comparisons that can uncover where the weakest links of these chains of events are and give your business the opportunity to proactively correct it.

By taking a closer look at each link, trending can identify where the sales efforts should be more focused to increase the success rate of the end sale. For example, if everyone that walks into your store buys something, but there were only two people a day in your business and your price is not a factor, what sales stage in the pipeline would you look at to turn a larger profit margin? You would want to look at the beginning, because you do not have enough people coming into your doors or inquiring about your product. So to increase traffic and awareness, you would want to do more outside marketing initiatives.

Now, say that you have two people every hour wanting to buy your business unit's widgets, but you cannot sell them to those clients because they are not ready yet. What sale stage would your sales pipeline problem be in? It would be toward the end. But, instead of the problem being in your sales ability to move customers through to the end, you now have an operational problem of having too few ready widgets on hand to supply the demand. By installing sale stages from the initial contact or inquiry (far left), the follow-up, pending sale, and then to the final sale (far right), your business unit can locate situations within your sales pipeline that are constricting the flow of revenue, thus an opportunity to make larger profits.

Your sales pipeline should look like a skinny triangle on its side:

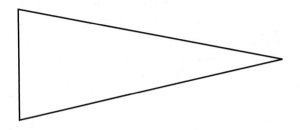

You must have considerably more inquires at the start of your pipeline (far left side), because your pipeline constricts as you move through each different sales stages, until you get to the purchase phase (far right side). Fall off from initial inquiry to the sale is due to many different factors. Most business units do not have every inquiry about their product turn into a sale, so this constriction factor occurs everywhere. Let's say that out of every ten inquires, you make one sale. To make your goal of ten sales, you must have one hundred inquires. Therefore, you have a 90% reduction from the opening of the sales pipeline (far left side) to the end (far right side).

With or without installing sales stages, if your business unit cannot tell where new customers are coming from, your marketing dollars are being spent blindly and without regard to a return on an investment. Source-of-business reports accomplish just that. These reports verify which marketing channels are growing revenue and which are not. A source-of-business report can be as simple as putting a marketing code at the bottom of your flyer and when customers call, asking them what the code at the bottom says, recording that proprietary code, and reporting the results at the end of that marketing campaign or these reports cause very complicated when performing beta testing for an online marketing blitz, search engine optimization placement, and/or a pay-per-click campaign. A source-of-business report can also have complex programs within each sales stages for possible evaluation as a link in the chain for a sale to transpire. By installing both sales stages and source-of-business reports into your management review of the sales operations and marketing dollars spent, sales pipeline management abilities will show trending and opportunities to change the business unit's strategy for greater profitability by spotlighting the movement of potential clients from their initial inquiry into the purchasing phase and also which marketing campaigns were most successful at putting them into that initial inquiry.

ASK FOR THE SALE AND PRESUME THE CLOSE, "WOULD YOU LIKE TO MAKE A RESERVATION TODAY?"

When you call a hotel and ask about room rates and availability, your call is not just considered an inquiry. The hotel makes a presumption that you will make the reservation and will ask you, "Would you like to make a reservation today?" That is why they lead you through the reservation sell screen (asking for critical information from you) to close the sale, before they answer a few basic questions (which is all that you wanted in the beginning). The hotel personnel are trained to always ask for the sale and presume that they will close the call and give you a confirmation number at the end of that call for a reservation.

You can market a product line until you are blue in the face, but if you never ask for the sale, you will not sell very much and cause the sales cycle period to lengthen from the initial contact to the final purchase. At the end of every sales opportunity, which in this "ask-for-the-sale" mind-set is always, you will say something like, "May I earn your business today?" "Would you like to make a commitment to that item today?" "Would you like to become our customer by doing 'X' today?" or "What will it take for you to purchase this item today?" These are just some of the questions that should be included in your everyday dialogue when your mind-set is in the "ask for the sale" mode.

Furthermore, when you presume the close within your sales presentation, it is just a matter of time or when they are going to buy from you. This mind-set overcomes the salesperson's worries about the rejection moment and frees them up to build a sales relationship, which in turn can foster a long-term sales commitment from that customer. Just think of expanding that way of thinking (ask for the sale and presume the close) to each of the associates that have the potential to make a sale within your business unit.

Every person with whom those associates communicate on a potential customer level, their mode of thinking, *How many widgets and when would you like them?* is now installed in their mind-set. How many more sales could your business unit produce?

Training the associates within your business unit to ask for the sale will be more difficult to do if you do not also train them on presuming the close, since the fear of rejection comes into play. Presuming the close alleviates that fear. Start the training off slow in the most visible departments of customer purchasing contact opportunities, and then expand upon that radius to include everyone that could make a sale for your business unit, *which is everyone in your business unit.*

This training will soon become a culture, producing increased purchases and shorter sales cycles from initial contact to final commitment and also make your business unit more proactive in the sales process.

SALES BLITZING AND ACCOUNT MANAGEMENT TECHNIQUES

When your business unit wants to launch a new product line and/or reintroduce the marketplace to a pre-existing product line in a short period of time, one effective method for this message delivery within the hotel business is to conduct a sales blitz.

A sales blitz for a hotel consists of gathering as many "foot soldiers" of the "sales army" as possible and assigning zones within a certain territory of that hotel's primary feeder business locations for them to visit for new business and leaving some form of informational kit/collateral on the hotel's product line with those businesses. This information from the blitz is usually left with an HR representative, economic decision maker, frontline gatekeeper, and so on. From there, the sales blitz member is to collect as much information on that stop from that prospect on a list of pre-set, pre-qualifying business needs from a hotel as they can within that five to ten minute time span, and then go off to the next "door of opportunity." Within the sales hours of nine a.m. until five p.m., the average person within the blitzing team wants to accomplish thirty-five to fifty sales calls.

Let's say that you had ten people sales blitzing, all doing forty sales stops in a day, for three days. Your business unit's sales blitz would produce 1,200 person-to-person product line sales calls in a short time span of three days. *Wow*!

The key to a successful sales blitz is that by asking a few pre-qualifying questions within those five to ten minute sale stops, new leads can be generated for immediate follow-up by someone on day two, three, four, and so on. What does this person do on day one, when not following up on leads on those remaining days? That person calls on the top twenty accounts on the first day as a courtesy call and if they finish with those top twenty stops, they go out and find business leads in the secondary zones to make spot blitzing attempts.

There are many forms of sales blitzing: themed blitzes, blitzes ramping up to grand openings, super prize giveaways, drawings, and many more. But the core feature of any sales blitz is to personally "knock" on as many doors, gather new business generation leads, and download product line information to those leads as quickly as possible for immediate follow-up and sales closing. With sales blitzing, you have a contact person's information and a reason for the sales follow-up, thus your sales process can begin and create more opportunities for revenue growth.

COLD AND WARM CALLING

What is the difference in a cold or warm sales call? The big difference is that with a warm sales call, you have a trace file established on the contact that has pre-qualified information needed to sell your product line to them and you are now following up for an initial or repeat sale. On a cold call, you have no knowledge, except the company's main contact information, and from there you must uncover facts, contacts, detailed information, wants and needs, likes and dislikes, and buying patterns, all to make a sales presentation to them. Please note each client may require that you record and learn more than those items listed above for a sale to progress. This process may take several warm call attempts to accomplish the sale, which is what a good salesperson excels at—follow-up.

Success occurs when you go back to the basic cold calling action plan within your sales and marketing strategies for generating new leads for the business unit. Cold and warm calling is like a "cart before the horse" theory. You cannot make a warm call until a cold call is done, so this is why the objective in studying a pipeline approach to your sales success needs to focus first on how many cold calls were done and converted into warm calls. If you start producing more cold calls to fill your sales pipeline from the start, more sales will come out at the end!

PENETRATION AND SATURATION OF A CUSTOMER'S ACCOUNT

What are your top twenty accounts? Have you made sure that every possible amount of business within those clients is being obtained from them? Penetration and saturation sales techniques complement the 80/20 theory, which says that 80% of your business comes from 20% of your clients. This ensures a factor of total market share capturing of your clients' finite dollars spent on any one product line.

Penetration techniques involve networking, uncovering, and drilling down within a company to make sure that all departments are knowledgeable about your product line's already established business relationship with that client at some other level. It also assumes that you can support all of their purchasing wants and needs based upon your product line's pre-established capabilities and deliverance. A penetrating sales approach follows a company's organizational chart like a roadmap, driving the sales pitches down from the top of it, all of the way to the last supervisory layer, and uncovering new business along the way. This is what penetration sales is all about.

Think of a penetration sales technique as a tree that you see in the field. It is just one tree, but how many branches, twigs, leafs, roots are there to that one tree, and have you made sure that you have asked for the sale from each and every one of those locations within that one tree for your product?

On the other side of the coin is saturation. Saturation techniques involve making sure that all departments have not forgotten about your business and that they have an awareness about your product, so you are their first call to purchase from. Think of a saturation sales technique as a sponge. After you dunk it in water it is very wet, but if you wait three days with no water added to that sponge, most of the water has evaporated. Wait another month with no water added to the sponge and all of the water will have evaporated, and it will be hard to use. The sponge (customer's account) must be continuously saturated with water (service awareness techniques) to stay wet (buying your product line first), or the first business unit called on to purchase from will not be yours.

By combining penetration and saturation sales techniques into your follow-up, a higher success rate in retention and sales from your current and future account base will occur.

KNOW WHAT THE "JONESES" ARE DOING

Knowledge is power, and it must be a cornerstone of understanding for operational and sales success against your current and future competitive set. Do you know what your competition is doing right now to market and operationally produce a similar product line? Do you know what cross-selling potential your competition is aligning itself with for greater sales growth? Do you know what improvements from an operational, administrative, sales and marketing, and management approach your competition is going to make, thus shifting higher demand for it? Do you know who is going to become a competitor for your customer's finite dollars and erode your market share? I am not asking you to predict the future, but I am asking you to take stock and know about your competition as well as you know about your own product line, from a customer's viewpoint.

The only way to defend competition from taking your business and allow you to grow your revenue is to have a better product line, know how to market it more effectively, know your strengths and weaknesses compared to other product lines, know what changes your business unit is going to make to protect itself from a threat from the competition's product line, know the marketplace and forecast trend opportunities, know that you truly do have an "apples to apples" product line compared to the competitors, know what changes are needed to make it run more operationally smooth and make sales more effective, and know what success and failures your competition is enduring. Most importantly, you must know the *why* to all of the above questions!

Having knowledge of all of these above issues is what is meant by knowing what the Joneses are doing. Start learning about the "Joneses" today, or be prepared to be bought or sent out of business by one of those "Joneses" tomorrow.

SHARE SHIFTING

Share shifting is a term that hoteliers use to describe moving a client base from their competition, to them. Share shifting is not getting *new* businesses to try your product line (a hotel in this example); it is taking a current client database (clients already having hotel needs and currently using other hotels) and moving it to your database (they stay at your hotel). As discussed earlier in this book, there are "X" dollars spent on any product line at any one time. The objective within share-shift marketing is to move more of those finite dollars spent on any product line into your business unit. You will be going for a bigger slice of the pie, but it is still just one pie that has not gotten any larger, just your portion of it has.

You need one of two things in place to sell any item: the clients either want or need your product line or a combination of both. Without a want or need from the client, you cannot sell much of anything to anyone. So, the advantages of share shifting over getting new customers/clients are:

- The want and need are pre-established

- The client is already buying, so spending habits are historic, thus forecasting can be done for pre-qualifying their future spending consumption

- Having purchased from your competitor in the past, selling strategies on your product line's advantages over your competition can be highlighted and exploited

- A pre-qualified database for quicker sales effectiveness, ramp up/your "low hanging fruit"

- Builds revenues in a soft or downward trending marketplace

- No wasted time on "uncovering" needs in your sales stage progression. Due to this, you can move the client quicker through the sales pipeline to the purchase phase

With share-shift marketing, your top-line growth will be faster than with most other sales campaigns, due to the fact that you have an accelerated cycle

THE PROFIT REPAIRMAN®

built into this sales effort. So, go on out there and get a bigger piece of that market share pie, before someone else does and then throws it in your face.

OCCUPANCY TO A.D.R—FINDING YOUR PERFECT REV.PAR

Occupancy in your business unit could mean the proportion of widgets sold to the total number of widgets available for sale. *A.D.R* could mean your total sold widgets revenue divided by the number of widgets sold that made up that total revenue.

I discussed occupancy, *A.D.R*, and *REV.PAR* earlier, but I wanted to touch on these items in a different light. *REV.PAR* (revenue per available room) is made up of occupancy (how many rooms were sold, divided by the entire amount of rooms available for sale, which comes to an occupancy percentage) multiplied by *A.D.R* (average daily rate—all room revenue added up and then divided by the number of rooms sold that made up that revenue, which comes to a said dollar amount). Simple math says that the *occupancy* percentage multiplied by *A.D.R* equals *REV.PAR* (which equals a dollar amount, for example: 72% occupancy times an $82.10 *A.D.R* equals a *REV.PAR* of $59.11). In a hotel, managers have to make sure that the blending of these two variables that make up *REV.PAR* are optimized daily in order to maximize revenue opportunities; the same is also true in your business unit.

Let's say Business A has only one hundred widgets in stock today to sell and sold all one hundred of those widgets at one dollar a piece, and Business B has only one hundred widgets in stock today to sell and sold fifty widgets at two dollars a piece. Which business had more top-line sales? Neither, they are equal in top-line sales with one hundred dollars, but not in bottom-line profit potential. Why? Because Business B now has fifty more widgets to sell (or a potential of up to one hundred more dollars in sales if they sold their remaining widgets at two dollars a piece) and only paid the variable expense costs on fifty widgets to get the same top-line sales as Business A with one hundred widgets sold.

This example would be true if all things were equal: supply, demand, and price point. Now, let's say that Business B learns that Business A has sold all of its one hundred widgets for that day, and Business B has the last fifty widgets left in town to sell, but the demand is for sixty more widgets today. Should Business B raise their price, knowing that the demand for widgets today is over the supply? Can the optimal price point rise because of this factor? *Yes*, that is what finding your perfect *REV.PAR* means to your business unit—finding out how to make the most money from your supply.

Selling all of your supply at the lowest rate every day is not always the best solution, because you are incurring the variable expense to drive those sales and wearing down the operational functions of that business unit for those sales, when on the other hand, you could have lowered sales by raising the price slightly, thus creating an opportunity to blend price and supply to the current demand and provide more bottom-line profit potentials for your business unit.

When is the last time you looked at the perfect *REV.PAR* for your business unit's situation? Is your product priced too low or too high? Do you have too much or not enough supply? How is your demand? Could you mix the number of items sold and the sales price together and make more money than your current top-line revenue strategy? Go out and find your business unit's perfect *REV.PAR*, and along the way, you may just increase your bottom-line profit potential and send it to a higher level of achievement. Or, once again, *call me*, I can help!

PERFORM WEEKLY AND MONTHLY SALES AND MARKETING REPORTS

To make sure that your sales efforts are heading in the right direction, perform weekly and monthly sales and marketing reports regarding your business unit's past sales initiatives for future sales achievement. "*Without movement in the water, no waves will ever hit the shore,*" and a weekly and monthly report can justify that enough sales movement was performed (waves in the water) to continue the trending of future sales (hitting the shore). Some of the questions asked in the hotel business to a salesperson weekly are the following and focus on the micro part of the sales pipeline:

> What are your tasks and statistics for each market segment?
>
> Who generated the top ten room nights this week?
>
> What is your action plan for next week?
>
> Were there any challenges faced in your sales efforts?

> What is your most important task to do next week, and how are you going to accomplish it?
>
> Who is new in your database for this last week?
>
> List any other factors that led to your successes or non-successes this week.

Following are some of the directives given in the hotel business to a salesperson monthly that they need to respond to, and they focus on both the micro and macro part of the sales pipeline.

> Propose rates per segment that will contribute to the hotel's future success.
>
> Estimate annual top-line room revenue for the next twelve months.
>
> Provide a commentary on the central reservation production vs. property direct bookings.
>
> What are next month's objectives, with specific and measurable goals within each target market?

> Provide a list of the top twenty accounts and list why, if any, was there movement within those rankings.
>
> What is next month's action plan on sales activities, marketing initiatives, and yield management strategies?

No matter what it says or how the format of your business unit's sales reports look, the reporting out on the sales activity and interactively reviewing it with the sales department weekly and monthly will allow for a better understanding of where you were, what you did to get where you are now, and where you are going. Remember, sales reports are a perfect time for both the operations and sales departments to effectively communicate with one another, celebrate successes, figure out how to overcome the non-successes of the past, and ensure a better outcome in the future. Start today and let your sales report bring your company one step closer to your goals.

REPEAT CUSTOMER LOYALTY PROGRAMS AND REWARD CLUBS

Attracting new customers takes more money than retaining the current ones. Some businesses comment that it takes eight or more times the marketing dollars needed to acquire new customers than to maintain pre-existing ones.

One way to retain a loyal customer base is through repeat customer loyalty programs and reward clubs. The hotel business has had these repeat customer loyalty programs and reward clubs installed for over thirty years, calling it a "frequent stay club memberships." These programs have driven an amazing amount of brand loyalty (room nights sold) and higher customer satisfaction ratings over the years. Today's hotel frequent stay club membership rewards come in all forms and promotions, but at the heart of these programs is the theory that it costs less to retain than to attract customers. Repeat customer loyalty programs and reward clubs work under the 80/20 theory to retain their top 20% of clients. This may not be 100% true in your business unit's case, but it leads into the thought that your current clients are acutely more valuable to your bottom line than what your new customers could be. No matter what your revenue stream's marketing mix, maintaining a higher retention of your customers that offer your business a repeat purchase opportunity can only help your net operating income.

Another great reason to install some sort of repeat customer loyalty program and reward club are for the capturing of valuable database information from your clients that can generate the following: buying trends, statistical data, satisfaction indexing feedback, a sense of fraternalism (belonging to a group, associated with members, recognized by others), customer relationship management, program analysis, and operational and sales initiatives.

What does your business unit do for repeat orders from long-standing customers? Do you know who your top twenty clients are? Do you know what your client's wants and needs are for their buying decisions to take place? Do you know how much client "X" has bought from you in the last five years combined, and how much over the last six months, what is their trend? One way to start answering these and many more questions is through a repeat customer loyalty program and reward club.

FIND WHAT MAKES YOU DIFFERENT, "EVERYBODY HAS A BED TO SLEEP ON"

In the hotel business, everybody has a bed to sleep on and a shower to use. To stand out from the rest of the competition, a hotel must find out what makes them different from their competition and create marketing campaigns around those differences.

There must be differences in hotels, or why else could you be charged anywhere from $40 to $200 for a bed to sleep on and a shower to use from any given hotel, all on the same interstate exit? In fact, some hotels charge over $10,000 a night. Are their beds and showers that much better? Do they truly offer twice as much more than a $5,000 a night room, or is it that they market to consumers in a way that creates that pricing demand by having their differences so much greater from that of their competition and the perception of it within those customers' mind-sets?

What makes your product line different from that of your competition? Write down what you think in the space provided on the next pages and include visual and non-visual aspects, concrete and abstract items, what you think your perceived and non-perceived values are, strengths and weaknesses, pricing structure(s), anything you think is relevant, and finally, your gut feeling why your product line is different from that of your competition.

My product line is different from my competition because:

Visual and Non-Visual Aspects

_____
_____
_____

Concrete and Abstract Items

_____
_____
_____

Perceived and Non-Perceived Values

_____
_____
_____

Strengths and Weaknesses

_____
_____
_____

Pricing Structure(s)

_____
_____
_____

Anything that is Relevant

_____
_____
_____

Gut Feeling

_____
_____
_____

Extra

_____
_____
_____

How are you different? Now, focus your marketing efforts to exploit that gap between those differences in you and your competitor's product line.

Marketing to your differences from your competition will set you apart in the mind of the consumers for their purchasing decisions and create an individual identity within tight marketplaces where similar product lines compete for the finite dollar supply, make a larger retention rate available, and will relieve some of the burden on the sales force for increasing the new customer acquisition rate.

SELL VALUE, NOT PRICE

If you were to sell value and not price for your product line, the optimal pricing point could not be raised, because in a true supply-and-demand model, value is nothing, but to humans, value means that there is an emotional connection and that can yield to higher pricing and profits.

In this ever price-driven economy that we live in, having your product line attach an emotional tag to current and potential customers will help maintain, among other things, your price integrity and brand loyalty. A value is an overall feeling from the customer on their dollars spent for your product line and cannot be defined with exact boundaries. Due to value selling, this emotional connection with consumers on their dollars spent can yield pricing flexibility beyond what the true supply-and-demand model says that your product line's optimal price point should be.

When you focus on selling the value of your product line and not just the price, you can evaluate your customers' buying decisions on more than the level of price alone. When value selling occurs, the study of the buying decisions for your customers can expand into questions of perceived value, price to product and the delivery of it, brand recognition and the value associated with it, consistency in product and service quality, customer expectation achievement, ways that you can improve, and the overall experience with the purchase.

Price is a yes or no answer, but value can deliver the answers of yes, no, or maybe, and adding those maybes from clients' replies yields more sales results in the end.

If you only sell price in your product line, some customers will jump from product to product because they take only a price-driven consideration into account. When this happens, you have nothing to offer them but that price, thus, you cannot build any loyalty within that individual, so when your price is higher, the sale from that price-driven customer is lost, with no recovery available.

But, when you value sell to a customer, you have an array of fallback sale strategy options to retain customers; if that one piece of the value pie is cut out (like price), you can now refocus on the others. By value selling, you build loyalty, higher price point considerations, share-shift marketing opportunities become available, added multi-layer sales strategy possibilities form, and assistance in maintaining price integrity within economic downward trending times can occur.

By the way, I hope that you see the *value* in this book, not just the *price*. *If not, please contact me; you have a partner in helping your business' success rate, not just another book by another author to read and then put on the shelf!*

AMENITY SELLING

In the hotel industry, they talk about amenity selling because amenities can set a hotel apart from its competition's price point, because, as we mentioned earlier, a hotel's core product (the bed and shower) functions the same as most everyone else's. But, when you sell your core product with amenities wrapped around it, the opportunity for rate variation and "apples to oranges" comparison selling exists within the marketplace. Amenity selling is a perceived value, not concrete, that can lead to greater revenue opportunities from your client base.

For example, a majority of hotel customers can quickly compare room rates at one hotel to the room rates at another hotel, but a hotel's customers' estimation varies greatly on the dollar amount that they will pay for items like turn-down service, indoor pool, *Wi-Fi*, free breakfast, express check in/out, frequent stay clubs, tennis courts, theme decorations, amusement/water parks, ocean/beachfront views, twenty-four-hour restaurant, spa, golf course, casino, shopping outlets, location of the hotel, bars, etc. These are all examples of amenities that wrap around the core product (the bed and shower) that raise room rates and cause variation within the same product line and competitive set. Studies show that most amenities in a hotel are rarely used to their full capacity, but are paid for by all, with increased room rates past the true bottom-line margin needed to sell that core product line, which can be created through amenity selling more than just simply pricing the product alone. Amenity selling is primarily for customer selling, but you can also utilize its secondary benefits in the HR model for attracting new associates and retaining existing ones by offering more than your competitors' workplace environments can to those associates.

What about roadside assistance plans from the auto makers, another amenity? What about the fast food industry, have they not sold us on an amenity we call the drive thru? What about the emerging use of accepting debit cards as payment in businesses (flexible payment options) around someone's core product line? What about the laundry detergent bottles that have a "no-mess bottle?" Just one more example in a long list of products that sell amenities wrapped around their core product line.

Look all around and you can see that most businesses have an amenity to sell in one form and fashion, but have you really put great thought into amenity selling for your marketing campaigns to increase your pricing points and acquire more customers? Probably not, but why? Examine your business unit's amenities that are in place now, and what could be added, so you could wrap them around your core product line to create rate variations within your marketplace and gain greater market share, thus growing your profit.

TOP OF MIND AWARENESS AND BRAND RECOGNITION

Millions and millions of dollars a year from every industry and various product lines are spent to perform these above functions. Do you? No, not spend millions of dollars, but do you incorporate top of mind awareness and brand recognition within every one of your sales and marketing calls?

Building top of mind awareness and brand recognition can be costly, but it can also be as simple as putting your logo and contact information on everything that a client receives when doing business with you. Go find your happy medium, but find it you must. If not, almost half of your effective message is lost the same day you deliver it to a client, and the rest of your selling message goes shortly after that.

I want you to conduct a poll for your business unit's product line. Call your clients, vendors, associates, and some individuals off the street and ask them what's the first thing they think about when you say "X" (something associated with your product line). Then ask them what your company does. Be prepared to be shocked, because you cannot expect to build new and repeat customer orders without having any top of mind awareness and brand recognition. Look at your sales message; is it clear, concise, and repetitive? If not, refocus the sales approach on the two key factors that can keep and attract new customers: top of mind awareness and brand recognition.

Another approach to remember about building your top-line sales growth is co-branding. How many product lines are out there in the marketplace that would be non-intrusive, complementary, or have a positive impact on the buying decision of a customer regarding your product line? A lot! All of those product lines mentioned above have a database of customers, and so do you. Why not work up an agreement between your business unit and theirs and cross promote, advertise, solicit, market, and bring visibility to each other's product lines for share-shifting opportunities from each other's competitive set?

Co-branding can also lower costs, offer more product line access to your clients, and prospect to a more qualified database in less time. In the hotel business, everything from the preferred credit card to long-distance service provider is co-branded. What are you waiting for with your product line? Someone to call you? Co-brand your product line today with top-of-mind awareness that has brand recognition to yield greater sales growth for your tomorrows to come.

PACKAGING

Packaging is a way to put together isolated individual pieces of different, but complementary/non-intrusive products into a whole new product line, which increases the value of the sum, creates a marketing niche and a wider client base to conceal the hard costs of each individual item, and in turn, lowers the time consumption of selling each component separately, which adds to the "convenience factor" for up-selling capabilities to the consumer.

Packaging comes in all forms and sizes, from perfume to exotic vacations and everywhere in the middle. If your product line can be packaged, it will have increased visibility from the cross-promoted items that are included in that new package and have exposure to a broader client base for those cross-promoted product lines. Potential customers can now experience your product from your business unit using a soft sales approach for the consumer purchasing decision. Find out who, what, and where your product line can be included into packages and supply those industries with your product line.

Let's say you own a company that sells pool chemicals. Could you not get together a package to sell to customers that would include pool chemicals, weekly testing/cleaning and chemical regulation of the pool, with pool toys for the family and call it "The Pool Owner's Package"?

What about having a business in the retail industry? If you owned a cigar shop, could you not put together a package for cigar lovers that each month they would receive one of "X" number of cigars from around different parts of the world, delivered directly to their house? Packaging can be done with almost any product line and season. Remember when doing packages to bring a theme or branding to that package so all the items are connected in some small way to one another in the mind of the consumer.

When you start to look at all of the marketing channels available for your product through packaging, you will start to think outside of your regular client parameters. Packaging will serve you and your business unit with increased sales potential and generate exposure to a much broader range of potential future clients.

RADICAL SALES AND MARKETING

The meaning of the adjective radical is "not bound by traditional ways or beliefs." Here are the "must dos" of a seasoned business unit's radical salesperson and marketer.

No stone goes unturned in your search for new leads and clients; no sales idea is too silly or stupid to try; you sell to everyone, every day, no matter what their size; you sell more than you market; you utilize yield management techniques; you just do not leave collateral, you collect a database for follow-up; you go down swinging and then get back up for another round; you are always in "selling mode;" you network, not just talk to people; you are "it," no one but you can make it happen; when you fail, you succeed by learning from it; you start your day with a goal and focus on its achievement; you look for ways to sell to prospects that others are not; you carry your business cards with you everywhere; wherever you go you see a future client, no matter how many no's they have given you; you write down phone numbers from passing businesses on the street; you see customer obstacles as an opportunity to get testimonial referrals from them by exceeding their expectations; you work on the probability theory; you radiate confidence and bring direction to clients; you take ownership of your sales 100%; you are out finding new revenue generation that your competition never knew existed and selling to them before they do; you see doors of opportunities, not slammed ones in your face; you are asking for the sale every time, in all possible ways, with each client you communicate with; you are a relentless "door knocker" and grass roots marketer; you look at your sales reports for new business that purchased from you; you drive the desire and passion for each sale with every presentation; you fight tooth and nail to retain a client and make new ones every day when you come into work; you smile until it hurts just to go to bed and wake up to attack your business leads all over again tomorrow.

Are you ready for the challenge? Are you ready to become a radical salesperson and marketer for your business unit? Why not? Are you afraid to get a little emotional about your sales and marketing? Only emotional selling sells to clients on a regular basis with consistency. No one wants an order taker in their sales department; your product line is not that special to afford you that luxury. If you are not emotional about the product line that you represent, your sales will never reach full capacity.

Keep it (sales and marketing campaigns) simple (*KIS* theory) for the biggest bang with the fewest bucks! Oh, by the way, the above sentence is the longest sentence in this book. Do you know the reason why? Because it is aggressive and unconventional and "not bound by traditional ways or beliefs," just like what a radical sales and marketer for your business unit needs to be.

Go be radical today!

CHAPTER 3
"∞" HUMAN RESOURCES

LABOR EFFICIENCY MODELING

Getting yourself and your business unit into the mind-set of thinking about labor efficiency modeling is one of the keys to running a profitable business.

The last time you looked at your current standards was when? Do you know what the correct production efficiency from each of your job codes is, even yours? What is your monitoring frequency? Are your efficiency modeling standards relative and timely with the current work force, market conditions, pricing structure, technology, and machinery in place? When do unacceptable results on each end of the parameter's spectrum trigger that an adjustment needs be made?

Do you share your statistical results from the modeling output calculation with the associates, HR, and supervisors for constructive assimilation and benchmark performance managing? You cannot tell someone to do better at something if you cannot show them why and where they are not meeting standards. Are you making labor efficiency part of the corporate culture and driving performance, retention, rewards, and career paths with them? Is your monitoring on efficiency placed upon the greatest job code that will yield the highest returns? Can your associates deliver upon current standards without task saturation overcoming them and quality being affected?

All of the answers to these above questions and more, along with revenue and greater efficiency, can be generated when you apply labor efficiency modeling to your business unit. Always focus your labor efficiency modeling to the greatest payroll burden and work backwards throughout your business unit as you are re-implementing your standards.

How do hotels use labor efficiency? One way is in the form of cleaning rooms, the "minutes per room" or *M.P.R.* that it takes a room attendant to clean a room. At the end of that workday, all of the time from a room attendant is added up and then verified that it fits within the "minutes per room" standards for all of the rooms that were assigned to them for cleaning. When these numbers are reviewed, deviations can be determined that very day, so corrective action can be taken to balance out the week's labor efficiency model before the overages hit a profit and loss statement. Labor costs on cleaning rooms can greatly impact the bottom line of a hotel, so that is why daily monitoring of this labor cost component (labor efficiency) helps a hotel bring down the appropriate payroll percentages and budget adherence is achieved.

Labor efficiency modeling can bring great success to your business unit if implemented successfully. What does your labor efficiency look like and how are you going to make it better?

CORRECTLY ON-BOARDING NEW ASSOCIATES AND PIPELINE CANDIDATES

What is one of the fastest ways to increase HR expenses and create workflow stoppages? On-boarding new associates incorrectly and not having enough candidates in your HR pipeline, that's how. "You never get a second chance to make a first impression." The precedent is set on the very first day of a new hire's career with your business unit. Whether they are digging ditches or filling out paperwork and watching videos, the company's professionalism, operating procedures, the employer's commitment to its associates, and the overall workplace experience is entrenched within the mind-set of that new associate within those first few weeks.

Do you have a standardized, detailed, 0–90 day on-boarding action plan in place with performance metrics and benchmark accomplishments for correctly evaluating the progression of all new associates and transitioning them into long-term team members? Do you throw new hires to the "sharks" or provide support platforms to them in the form of training (all media and hands-on types), coaching, mentoring, monitoring, corrective actions for redirecting, *S.O.P.*s, support (technical and non-technical), and progress measurement indicators?

Go look at the last two years of associate turnover in their first ninety days of employment with your business unit and understand the reasons *why*. Once you find the whys, you can identify the missing steps of the on-boarding process. After those system steps have been reorganized, look at what steps should be created for the future to produce a better on-boarding system. Why would you do that? Because, businesses will always have new hires and turnover, so this situation is not going away. In fact, as the marketplace grows tighter and tighter for good and qualified new hires, correctly on-boarding associates is a major factor in retention, lowering HR expenses, successful integration of them into the workflow, and converting them into long-term productive team members for the success of all.

Think of your business unit as if it were a basketball team (you would need five players to be fully staffed, playing the game of basketball, when pipelining candidates). Would you employ only five associates (all starters) and no one else on your team, or would you have extra players (associates) waiting in the wings to come in to the game off of the bench and play for those five players if they get hurt, foul out, need a rest, quit, or worse, get traded to another team? The answer to the above question would be no, unless you deliberately want to set your business unit up for failure in the beginning.

Life and things happen to your associates every day, voluntarily and in-voluntarily. You must be prepared for this on all levels of your business unit. One way on the HR front is to have candidates (current and non-current associates) in a hiring pipeline for those soon-to-be-open/heavy-turnover-rated positions, ready to move through the HR pipeline to fill the void left by "something" happening to one of your "starters" (associates).

Remember, an HR pipeline, similar to a sales pipeline, does not always mean that you have to retain someone on payroll, just in case. It can also refer to identifying someone who you can call upon to fill that HR vacancy within a short span of time and with as little disruption to the business unit as possible (in-house or not), a good database of resumes never hurt any business! As with all pipeline process approaches, you must continuously be filling the opening of the pipeline with excess amounts of potential candidates, so that the end result of this ever-moving, constricting pipeline is a successful transition between a new and old associate for those upcoming, voided positions.

Pipelining candidates means that the HR department is in a continuous, pro-active status and that they are offering solutions to your HR problem, more than, "I will put an ad it the paper and see what happens." The human resource department should never stop looking to "trade-up" on associate talent and reposition others for greater utilization within your business unit, and one successful way to achieve this is by having a full pipeline of candidates.

LOWERING ASSOCIATE TURNOVER BY HAVING A BONUS POTENTIAL

Turnover is not all bad to an organization. Attrition and greater efficiency can both individually or combined lead to lower staffing models, which in turn causes some turnover. But as a whole, associate turnover costs all businesses. No matter how small and for whatever positions that the turnover occurs within, an employer pays for it in the form of revenue optimization and expense accumulation. How do you lower the associate turnover rates?

First, you must find out the reason why the turnover is occurring. Second, you must really (I mean *really*) understand *why* turnover is occurring within your business unit. Please do not just look at the surface answers. Do some drilling down into the sub-surface and find out the real answers by job code, region, external factors, etc. Now that the "real" reasons why turnover is occurring have been identified, prioritize them by:

>The economics

>The social responsibility to the company's core values/mission statement

The HR structure for future operational and sales goal achievement

The elements of change that will be required to transform lower turnover rates

The time frame

The complete cost to benefit ratio analysis from internal to external factors

Bonuses are ways to accelerate movement and expand upon some outcome that a business unit deems critical to the success of a healthy bottom line. Why not use bonuses to also help lower your turnover rates?

Have you ever heard of the phrase, *Cash is king*? It means that no matter what, everyone appreciates cash rewards given to them from time to time. Since our economy is based on the use of currency for most transactions, if you have cash-induced bonuses, everyone can understand the value, measure its worth, and utilize that cash in some way and fashion.

Basing bonuses on performance is a must, but what about weighing the outcome of the whole bonus, based on service time, both length and placement within the calendar year?

When implementing a bonus structure, be it for lowering turnover or not, include these key factors:

> What is the most critical time of the year for operations and sales achievement?
>
> Is the bonus achievable, measurable, timely, and relevant to the outcome desired?
>
> Are payout frequency intervals short enough to maintain momentum between them?
>
> Can the business unit afford to pay out 100% achievement on it (worst-case scenario thinking) if everyone makes it?
>
> Do you have baseline budgets and stretch markers in place for overachievement?
>
> Is this bonus promoting performance without compromising the *S.O.P.*s, through operations or sales, both legally and ethically?

When you combine these above factors and then throw your bonus into your weighted average and service time, lower turnover rate patterns can start to appear. Just remember, *not all* turnover is bad for a business; make sure that the jobs with the lowest turnover rates are also with the associates that produce the most.

MANAGING ASSOCIATE PERFORMANCE

How do you manage associate performance? Just like you would manage driving a car. You need to know where you are at the start, where you want to be at the end, and a roadmap to help optimize the distance from point A to point B and receive some redirection in case you are off the path.

Managing associate performance can be in the form of written documentation for reporting the results, personal follow-up/open dialogue with that associate, constructive feedback, timely reviews, accurate assessments, direct and specific directional action tasks that have been accomplished, and what needs to be accomplished for future goal platforms.

Along with these items, you need assessment tools that determine upward mobility capabilities and strategic skills currently in place or underdeveloped ones needing attention, placement within current and ongoing organizational charts, open dialogue with direct supervisors, customer satisfaction scores (if applicable), and financial performance metrics (if applicable). By combining the information and resources above, you know where the associate is and where he wants to end up, so you are giving the associate a "roadmap" on how to get there, and he can now "drive" his own career achievement by daily, hands-on deliverance within the business unit's success structure.

Each associate has a different want and need from a workplace environment, but by assisting each to accomplish his end results by managing his performance from the very first day of employment to the end, both the associate and business unit will see the most productive outcome. Only when a business unit focuses on managing associate performance through each associate as an individual part of the whole and manages career path/performance markers to their individual goals, can the sum of all associates' efforts be combined into one goal for the achievement of the entire organization.

Start managing associate performance and doing the reporting on it today, because we are all connected and dependent on one another. Your success depends on other associate's within your business unit, and managing associate performance is one way to guide that success in the right direction. Remember, "We win as one!"

CHAPTER 4
"Ω" ACCOUNTING

COMPETITIVE SET INDEXING

Do you know how you are stacking up against your primary, secondary, and marketplace competitive set in revenue and other financial factors? In the hotel business, stacking up on revenue means how hotels are doing in occupancy, *A.D.R* (average daily rate), and *REV.PAR* (revenue per available room) against other hotels in their brand, tier, price range, location, and region.

In the hotel business, if you had an *A.D.R* of $105 and your competitive set had an *A.D.R* of $100, you would be indexing to their *A.D.R* at 105%. Any indexing number that a hotel receives that is higher than 100% is favorable and vice versa. These indexing reports come out daily, weekly, monthly, and yearly for hoteliers to review, and they inform them how they are doing on a "true scale of comparison" at running their top-line revenue against that of their competition.

For example, let's say that you are making twice as much money as last year. Is this a good thing? Yes, but what if your competitors were making three times as much money as last year? In that case, you would not be indexing favorably against them, and that competitive set indexing report could inform you and cause management actions to correct that situation.

It is just not good enough to know what your statistical performances are; you need to know how those stats compare to the competition that you're fighting for market share with. Just indexing high is also not a sign of profitability either. Blending your indexing reports with financial reporting offers a much clearer picture of where you stand as a business owner and manager than just monetary reporting can.

What is your indexing number on top-line sales against that of your competition, over or under 100%? Knowing this indexing number can help your business unit with implementing future pricing and operational modeling. I encourage you to spend some time today and investigate your own business unit's competitive set indexing so you can receive a better view of how your performance picture compares to that of your competition.

CLOSE YOUR BOOKS NIGHTLY

Did you know that hotels close their accounting books (guest ledgers, house accounts, departmental ledgers, accounts receivable, city ledger, and advanced deposit ledger) nightly? Why would hotels do that, you may ask. Because, nightly closing of their accounting books allow for immediate reconciliation, so a hotel can identify and correct posting errors/miscoded items, generate net revenue/ledger balances, and create daily statistical performance metrics for a more accurate analysis.

Would you like to be able to go into your business unit and have some current gauge of the income statement's profit position at a time frame when changes could be made to affect the final outcome, or would you rather wait for over two weeks after the month ends to find out that there was a negative bottom-line growth after you were not able to do anything about it?

Although nightly closing of your business unit's accounting books may not be as feasible for you as some other industries, the mind-set of it is not. Does your business unit have timely, up to date, and accurate accounting books for management to make critical business decisions with when they need the information the most? If not, you need to.

Soft accounting closes are not that challenging. Just make sure that outputted numbers are taken into consideration and everyone is aware that there is some "flex" in the numbers. In my judgment, something of a current financial picture is better than none at all.

If daily conditions, factors, and circumstances are "change agents" that determine a business unit's cash flow requirements and affect its bottom-line results, then would you not want to get some picture of how those "agents of change" are affecting the accounting statements in quicker time frames than the current ones in place now? Many of today's accounting software programs can immediately generate some sort of preliminary statements with the push of a button, so why have you not added that to your weekly operational review checklist? Your views on how to use accounting statements must be parallel with the real world views, *daily*, because the change that is driving the supply-and-demand grid around your business unit can be viewed through these statements.

This is ground level thinking for "big picture" successful business building. When the accounting department's mind-set is daily, not monthly, they can post entries and reconcile and produce partial statements on demand, they will now be up to speed with today's business needs.

You can make a difference in your business unit's financial success by having the mind-set that your books close nightly.

Hurry up and finish reading and close *this book* to be successful in your life, career, and increasing the success rate of small and mid-sized businesses!

BREAKING DOWN YOUR INCOME STATEMENTS

The above statement sums it all up. Do you study your profit and loss statements with detailed, thought-provoking analysis and have comparison relationships with percentages of or cost associated with certain line items to the whole and the variances within them?

In the hotel business, everything on the expense side (fixed or variable) is a cost per occupied room and/or a percentage of top-line revenue, so an in-depth understanding of expenses can be revealed for comparisons and the "why" factor can be generated. For example, a hotel sold 6,000 rooms in one month and its gas bill was $4,500; the cost per occupied room for that gas bill would be seventy-five cents ($4,500 gas bill/6,000 rooms sold *M.T.D.*). Once you have that number, the hotel can then compare those seventy-five cents to every month after that, to the cost per occupied room for their gas bill, because now the gas bill has been converted from a whole-dollar expense into a baseline of "room to room" expenses, on which to gauge successful cost containment. What if this same hotel sold 10,000 rooms the following month, and their gas bill was $7,200? Did the hotel's gas bill increase? Yes, by $2,700. But, did that hotel control its expenses relative to their rooms sold? Yes, because its cost per occupied room on that gas bill was actually seventy-two cents, (or three cents better per room on the gas bill for that month) compared to last month's gas bill of seventy-five cents per room.

The explanation of this cost reduction per rooms sold could be through the offset of fixed costs to the entire expense, (fixed expenses going down with more rooms sold until a certain point) or it could be a combination of controllable and non-controllable measures, such as good hotel operations, conservation programs, guests usage, cost per therm, warmer weather, increased insulation, doing more laundry at night, billing cycle changes, etc. The major benefit to take out of this above example is that now the hotel can see on a penny to penny per occupied room comparison that this $7,200 bill is lower in a true expense comparison model than the gas bill from the month before.

Now that this knowledge is solidified through the analysis, the hotel can find out why that gas bill's cost went from seventy-five to seventy-two cents and hopefully produce even lower expenses, depending on the fact that the lower cost per occupied room of seventy-two cents was created by controllable measures or some other predictable factor.

Through detailed analysis of the major items on your business unit's *P and L* statement of top line, labor, controllable expenses, and bottom line (*N.O.I.* with Cash Flow) and breaking them down into a percentage of top line or cost per "X," your business unit can have real gauges on the profitability and knowledge of a true comparison of numbers. With these items now revealed, the business unit can now dig into the "why" for the controllable and non-controllable factors that are affecting the costs and perform corrections or expansions on those items that can bring the greatest bottom-line benefit. Go analyze those *P and L's* today!

HAVE A DAILY STATISTICAL DATA SHEET WITH COMPARISONS

Do you know right this very moment what performance metrics your business unit is achieving? This kind of snapshot performance (daily snapshot) report is what we call a "house count" in the hotel business. Within a hotel's house count, hoteliers look at rooms rented, number of arrivals/check-outs/clean rooms, *A.D.R*, occupancy, and so on. Hotels see this "house count" report as the tool that contains important and volatile numbers, which must be reviewed on a regular and continuous basis for the hotel to achieve its successful expense adherence and revenue projection model.

What performance metrics do you want to monitor for your business unit on a continuous basis that are the most important and are very volatile for the achievement of operational and sales success? Also ask yourself what kind of precise micromanagement report you want, to whom should this report go, and when and how often should this report be viewed when determining your businesses function and achievement ability.

Once you have these questions answered, installing the *S.O.P.* to monitor this "house count" becomes second nature to the business unit and in turn will radiate the importance and acceptance from your associates that these are the metrics that will drive their business unit to success and acclaim.

On no more than a couple of 8½ x 11-inch pieces of paper, have a "snapshot" of the top five to ten critical statistical metrics that determine your business unit's success, available with comparisons for your daily morning review. If you do not have this report, you cannot be proactive in management. With a daily statistical data sheet/ "house count," you have the ability to spot trends, and thus, small corrections in the operations or sales can be initiated to neutralize the adverse effect of any negative component. When you have daily statistical sheets that are simple, to the point, and full of the "most critical" metrics that you need, you can guide your business unit daily, which will lead to greater achievements of the business unit's budget and stretch goals. Focus on managing your business unit today, so that today will be tomorrow and tomorrow will be your everything.

REPORT OUTS

Daily statistical reports help to guide you through the month but do not drill down to all necessary financial levels. What about after the fact, when all the dust has settled, and the final income statements are released and detailed operational and sales accountability is a must, what then? That is when report outs on income statements come into play.

THE PROFIT REPAIRMAN®

Make sure that the following items below are contained in your report outs, including variances and percentage changes within those numbers, on the four major income statement components: top line (gross revenue); labor; controllable and non-controllable expenses; and bottom line (*N.O.I.* with Cash Flow), (all numbers are accumulated and may be partial quarters or years, but each are equal to one another in their respective time frames):

> Month to Date (*MTD*)
>
> Quarter to Date (*QTD*)
>
> Year to Date (*YTD*)
>
> Current Month (*MTD*) Year over last Year Month (Example: Oct. 07 to Oct. 06)
>
> Current Quarter (*QTD*) Year over last Year Quarter (Example: Q4 of 07 to Q4 of 06)
>
> Year (*YTD*) over last Year (Example: *YTD*-2007 to *YTD*-2006)
>
> Month over Month (Example: Oct. 07 to Sep. 07)

Quarter over Quarter (Example: Q4 of 07 to Q3 of 07)

MTD, QTD, and *YTD* to budget and stretch goals with remaining/declining balances to reach each of those goals

Projected *MTD, QTD* and *YTD* numbers against budget and stretch goals

Trailing three month average

Trailing twelve month average

Trailing eighteen month average

Trailing three to five year average

Annualized *MTD, QTD* and *YTD* numbers

Don't forget, visually, graphs, charts, and color-coding all add to the accelerated ability to understand, pinpoint, and emphasize negative and positive trending within your report outs. Another great tool is to set parameters around each line item, so an exception report can be generated and quickly identified when numbers exceed those boundaries.

Please take everything with a grain of salt and do not forget that drowning yourself in numbers and piles of paperwork will not always be the solution. A piece of paper can say anything, just look at the reason congress installed the Sarbanes-Oxley Act. Stay focused on the "real operations and sales at hand," but use every tool around you to assist in top-line growth and operational efficiency.

EPILOGUE

Quick, close your eyes! Could you have read this book, driven a car, or functioned very effectively with your eyes closed?

My life-long mission is to open your eyes a little wider, so you can be more effective in driving your life and career, and increasing the success rate of small and mid-sized businesses, which is the backbone of a country's economy and future growth.

The Profit Repairman's® Goal is to:

Reach, Teach, and Send!

I want to *Reach* as many small and mid-sized businesses as I can.

I want to *Teach* every small and mid-sized business owner and associate, rock-solid, time-tested principles for their individual and company's success.

> *"And then, because words are meaningless without actions behind them..."*

I want to *Send* small and mid-sized businesses into motion with concrete, corrective action plans to implement *today*, so that the owners and associates have a tomorrow to look upon.

Embrace the element of change and continue to grow your leadership skills in life and your career, as you stop biting your nails and start sharpening your claws, while you run your business like a hotel.

Make it (do not have) a great day!

Sincerely,
Tom

Platinum, which began as a start-up company in 1995, built by Lynn Brewer and Tom Marquardt, has the following companies to serve all of your company's and organization's immediate needs for increasing success rates.

PLATINUM, INC.:

A full-service, complete total turnkey management system, accounting and consulting services on a long or short-term contract basis for various small and mid-sized businesses, which also houses the entire "My Little Black Book to Success," "Stop Biting Your Nails and Start Sharpening Your Claws," and "The Profit Repairman" product/service lines.

PLATINUM PEO RESOURCES, INC.:

A national leading marketer for several professional employer organizations, which provides small and mid-sized businesses of *all types*, with an integrated suite of services including: HR administration and operational functions, pay-as-you-go worker's compensation and property and casualty insurance programs, compliance with safety and risk management, payroll and tax administration, and associate benefits.

THE PROFIT REPAIRMAN®

Platinum's contact information is below:

11000 Metro Pkwy. Suite 9
Fort Myers, FL 33966
O: 239-561-2591
F: 239-561-3589

Lynn Brewer • Tom Marquardt

www.paygoworkerscomp.com
www.theprofitrepairman.com
lynnb@paygoworkerscomp.com
tomm@theprofitrepairman.com